THE ZERO F*CKS COOKBOOK

This book is for all the people who woke up one morning and realised they actually didn't give a fuck.

THE ZERO F*CKS COOKBOOK

BEST FOOD LEAST EFFORT —— YUMI STYNES

hardie grant books

WELCOME

I love food.

I love delicious morsels of comfort and luxury and I think about eating constantly. It's one of the great pleasures in my life, but here we go: I have zero fucks left to give to bullshit cooking that wastes time, creates work and adds a whole unnecessary level of wankery to otherwise honest food.

I say NO to smoking my own meat, making puff pastry, dealing with a pig's head or in any way taking time out of my own busy life to do bullshit things to food.

Most nights I cook to feed at least six, often more. My house is total chaos. It's a zoo. Often an extra person or two arrives at my dinner table with little warning and I have to improvise and figure it out, but don't get me wrong – I love it. It's been a lifelong desire that my table should be welcoming, that people can just drop in, that anyone can cop a feed.

But I want to have fun too. I want to enjoy my family and enjoy visitors and not be at the stove or head in fridge, impressing God-knows-who with some stupid-arse thing that tastes no better than a lovely slice of cucumber or a perfectly roasted potato. Here's the thing: so much food is inherently delicious and doesn't need a helluva lot of intervention. Cucumber? Cut it with a knife. Yum. Bread? Add butter. Delicious.

If I want wanky food I will happily go to a restaurant and pay for someone else's white peach vierge dressing or fermented koji butter. At home? I already gave my fucks away. My loved ones will eat. The food I make is delicious. And I'll cook it because it's easy. It's what you've gotta do when you're cooking with a sum total of zero fucks.

YUMI XX

THE ZERO F*CKS ORIGIN STORY

I used to want to be a chef.

Early on in my adult life I worked as a cook in a couple of pubs and resorts around Australia. Let me tell you from experience that this kind of work is sexy and exhilarating. There is adrenaline, swagger, and ego, and with your co-workers there's a physical dance of cooperation, coordination, and brute force. There is shouting, laughing, pressure and, at the heart of it all, the pursuit of the sensory pleasures of food.

I'm into it. I'm into going to restaurants and letting professionals – with all their swagger and skills – use their training to take shit next level. I dig it. This is why I pay money for meals ... and, I confess, it is a considerable ongoing investment.

So, when I see cooking shows and recipe books encouraging crazy amounts of work, fuss and perfectionism in the average home cook, I shake my head. THIS IS NOT FOR ME! Leave it to the chefs!

I had a breakthrough a few years ago when I was preparing food for a post-marathon barbecue. A bunch of runners were coming back to my place and would all be hungry. What to do? The miso marinade for barbecued eggplant I made was so easy that I couldn't quite believe it, and I had to resist the urge to add in complications! I realised that equating personal labour with the love and care I wanted to express was STUPID. You can give yourself permission to choose cooking that is easy, but still exalts the food and the eaters of the food! (The eggplant was a hit, by the way, and I still make it to this day – the recipe is on page 89.)

Zero Fucks is all about making the best food with the least amount of fuss. I say YES to beautiful ingredients, simply assembled. I say YES to eating things that make you feel good and I say YES to making them without stressing. I say YES, YES, YES to letting the natural flavour and goodness of food sing.

I say yes to shortcuts, hacks, tricks and pre-made. I say yes to sometimes using expensive ingredients. (This is Zero Fucks after all, not Zero Bucks.) But I also say yes to avoiding waste, yes to making healthy choices and yes to celebrating the marvel that is food.

The older I get, the fewer fucks I have spare. I give a fuck about my family, my friends, and my work. Everything else? Well that's what this is about.

SHOPPING WITH ZERO F*CKS

When I was a kid living in rural Victoria, sourcing Asian ingredients was a mission involving a 350-km drive to the big city (Melbourne), where we'd stay overnight with my Aunty Tasma and stock up on art, culture and food. I remember standing with my mum at the checkout of the inner-city Japanese grocer with my mouth hanging open: everything we got was so expensive and so precious. We'd cart our loot back to Swan Hill and my mum would ration things out – only one piece of seaweed per kid, no more!

I'm not interested in cooking with hard-to-find ingredients. And I don't have an exotic spice mart at my doorstep any more than you do. Luckily, nowadays mainstream supermarkets all over the country stock items we used to travel hours to buy. It's such a gift.

Here's the thing, everything in this book can be bought from a mainstream regular supermarket. So if you're looking through and thinking, 'Nope, I don't know where to get that', you might need to look a bit harder. It could be right there in front of you. As we say in my house, 'Have a grown-up look'. This applies to my friends, who mostly live in big cities but call me up to tell me, 'I don't know where to get Panko breadcrumbs!' To which I say, 'Have a grown-up look! The most average supermarket in suburbia stocks them.' And soy sauce. And miso paste, and mirin. Just have a good look and if you're stuck, ask someone who works there!

Most bottle shops sell sakè. Pre-made sauces like soba sauce are harder to come by – but every Asian grocer will stock them.

I also try to avoid ingredients that you use once and then clog your pantry for five years.

Don't get me wrong, I love pursuing food and odd ingredients like a mad horndog. But most of the time I don't have time. This book is for the most-of-the-time times. I want you to be able to use the staples you keep in your pantry, and if you happen to find a beautiful snapper, or some Jerusalem artichokes, then you'll know what to do with them.

A QUICK NOTE ON INGREDIENTS

Rice
I use regular short-grain white rice. My mum buys crazy expensive imported Japanese rice and swears she can taste the difference but it doesn't bother me. All my rice is grown in Australia.

Salted butter
Salted butter is the standard in this book (I can't taste the difference between food cooked with salted or unsalted butter, to be honest). I live in Sydney, Australia, and I leave mine out of the fridge except in the middle of summer. I can get away with this because I use it before it has time to go feral.

Soy sauce
I use a Japanese-style soy sauce, Kikkoman, for all my recipes. Chinese soy sauce has a very different taste – if you have some and want to use it, it will work in my fried rice (page 59).

Spring onions (scallions)
I mean the long, pencil-thin ones with a short white base and a long, dark-green tail, common to every supermarket, greengrocer and Asian foodmart.

Whipped garlic
Whipped garlic is a hack I discovered a few years ago in my local grocer. It's sold as 'Garlic Dip', can be found in the refrigerated section along with other dips and is basically a whipped blend of garlic, oil and nothing else. It doesn't taste like the manky minced garlic your mum used to buy in jars. This tastes exactly like garlic, but a little milder, and I mostly use it when I want a super-fine mince or can't be bothered crushing, chopping or grating. Use a tablespoon to replace a clove.

CHEAP VS EXPENSIVE INGREDIENTS

The most expensive ingredient is not always the best! For example, sometimes the cheapest bread is the best fit for a particular recipe. In others I specify 'use the best quality butter' or 'use great bacon'. This means 'buy the best you can afford and feel comfortable with'. Some recipes go better with cheaper ingredients, some with the top-shelf stuff. Other recipes do just cost a lot to make, for instance my Stained Glass Cake, Pecan Slice and – of course – Lobster Hand Rolls (pages 182, 153 and 127) all contain items that cost a fair bit when you add them up. I'm at peace with this. I don't buy jewellery, designer clothes or alcohol, so most of my splurging is on food.

ZERO F*CKS NEEDS

I recommend you have these things in your kitchen:

Kitchen scales

Stand mixer

Food processor

Measuring spoons

Measuring cups

Real pepper grinder

Mandoline slicer

Citrus zester

Good knife

SMART LABELLING

Kim Deal from the band The Pixies once said, 'If I had one piece of advice for musicians starting out it would be, always label your tapes.' I'm the same with food. You think you're going to remember what it is you're bagging up and sticking in the freezer but two weeks will go by and you will have no recollection of what that thing is. Make life easy for yourself. Keep a permanent marker in the plastic wrap drawer and label your food.

A NOTE ON READING THE RECIPE

I had a cooking epiphany a few years ago. I'd always loved to cook and loved the science and art of food but I had a lot of cooking failures. Too many! Why? Because I have always had a problem with authority.

I have never liked being told what to do, and even though it's completely bonkers, for this reason I found it near impossible to follow a recipe. I could follow it to a point, before I'd invariably get 'creative' and add my own embellishments, or 'Yumify' it.

Of course, this is a way to discover new things and express yourself. Yes. It's also a good way to fuck up some perfectly good food. So here are two things I now know with utter certainty to be true:

1. I have an excellent sense of taste and smell.
2. I care more about this book being right than you do.

With these facts in mind, please consider how carefully I have tested and measured each of these recipes before you decide to get creative. Just follow the damn instructions. Trust me. I have no interest in letting you down.

A NOTE ON TIMERS

Everyone has a timer on their phone and this is one of your greatest assets in the kitchen. Believe me, setting a timer cuts out a whole heap of unnecessary 'guesswork' from your cooking and will give you a bloody good headstart in making food perfect, every time. And I hate to say it, but the same goes for owning a set of kitchen scales and using them. I use mine daily. They weren't expensive and they have changed my life.

A NOTE ON BARBECUING

I love my barbecue (as you'll see on pages 76–109) but one mistake I always used to make when people came over was to let them take over the cooking while I did more important things like lying on the floor looking at my phone. If my friends couldn't follow instructions, then they tended to overcook the meat! In spite of the clarity of my instructions! Don't be like me and do all the work only to have it ruined by well-meaning idiots/loved ones who don't believe that you know how your own barbecue works. Mine is BLOODY HOT and will murder a steak given the chance.

ABSORPTION-METHOD COOKED RICE

Let's get rice right. You're an adult now, you need to be able to do it. Serves 5

Cooking time: 22 minutes | Prep time: 2 minutes, plus soaking

STEP ONE

When you decide you're having rice as part of dinner that night, even if it's 10 in the morning...

- Measure out the rice into your saucepan.
- Fill the saucepan with cold water from the tap.
- With a clean hand, swirl the water around six times.
- Tip the water into the garden (my mum swears this is the reason her plants thrive).
- Fill the saucepan again with cold water from the tap.
- Swirl the water in the opposite direction six times.
- Tip the water into the garden.
- Now add 600 ml (20½ fl oz) water to the saucepan so that it sits 1 cm (½ in) above the level of the rice.
- Put the lid on and leave.

STEP TWO

When dinner is half an hour away...

- Put the covered saucepan with the rice on a high heat.
- As soon as it boils, turn the heat to as low as it can go, then set a timer for 12 minutes.
- When the timer sounds, turn off the heat.
- Leave the lid on the rice until you are ready to eat.

400 G (14 OZ) SHORTGRAIN WHITE RICE

TIP

When your rice has cooled, store it in a zip-lock bag for maximum freshness. But if you have run out of fucks, just put the whole saucepan in the fridge until you are ready to use it. It will last for 3 days like this.

ZERO F*CKS WEEKNIGHTS

Meals are like pop music – there's a reason why we always want the new song, the new star, the new fad foods. We crave fresh things. However, there is a lot to be said for a regular repertoire of weeknight meals that doesn't strain your brain. Throw some things together, add heat, eat. But I find if I don't keep rejigging the repertoire, I start to hate it a bit. It's stale, like last year's hit song. Add these to your weeknight mixtape and I promise, you'll be singing along!

SOBA NOODLES

These noodles are a fair dinkum life-saver because the ingredients last forever in the pantry and they take only a few minutes to prepare. This is how I picture it: you've taken everyone to the beach for an after-school swim. It was only meant to take an hour but everyone was having so much fun that you decided to stay on longer. Now you've got them home and they're sunburnt and starving. What can you whip up in the time it takes for them to rinse the sand off their feet and hang out their towels? Serves 6

Cooking time: 5 minutes | Prep time: 5 minutes

Set out small, rice bowl–sized bowls, one per person, and add a tablespoon of the chopped spring onion to each. Have a colander ready in the sink and chopsticks out for everyone.

Unbundle the soba noodles and toss them into your biggest saucepan of boiling water.

Meanwhile, combine the soba sauce and water in a small saucepan and bring to a low simmer. Keep warm until required (if you really can't be bothered, you can skip this step and serve the sauce cold).

Check the noodles. The packet instructions are often indecipherable so you may not know how long to boil them for – just keep checking by fishing out individual strands and biting into them at the 2-minute mark, 3-minute mark, etc. You want the al dente bite to be cooked out – but only just! Rinse them in cold water, using your hands to toss the noodles under the tap until they feel completely cold.

Pour 60 ml (2 fl oz/¼ cup) of the warm soba sauce into each serving bowl. Pile the noodles into a large serving bowl and serve them up in the middle of the table. Each person helps themselves to a small amount of noodles, which they dip into the sauce and eat immediately.

3–4 SPRING ONIONS (SCALLIONS), GREEN PARTS ONLY, VERY FINELY CHOPPED

500 G (1 LB 2 OZ) SOBA NOODLES

200 ML (7 FL OZ) SOBA SAUCE

200 ML (7 FL OZ) WATER

TIPS

1. For first-timers it seems counter-intuitive to rinse the noodles in cold water after cooking – we are so used to wanting our noodles to be hot! Rinsing is a key step because a) the noodles are meant to be served cold and b) cold water washes the starch off the noodles and stops them congealing into one stiff lump.

2. Leftovers can be made into a salad with chopped-up snow peas (mangetout), grated carrot, finely chopped spring onion and a sprinkling of sesame seeds.

3. If you don't have spring onions to hand, finely diced onion or leek will work well here, too.

NAILED-IT CAULIFLOWER

It drives me nuts when a simple vegetable like cauliflower consistently tastes better in restaurants than when I cook it myself. I spent months frustrated, trying to get this right without using restaurant quantities of frying oil. I'm happy to say that eventually, after many attempts, I nailed it! Be warned: it shrinks down quite a bit, so if you're using this as a main you may need to double the quantity. Serve it as a side to roast meats or barbecued fish, or make it the star with pitta bread, hummus and tabouleh. Serves 4–6

Cooking time: 40 minutes | Prep time: 5 minutes

Preheat the oven to 175°C (345°F).

Heat the oil in a large heavy-based frying pan over a high heat.

Add the cauliflower to the pan, sprinkle over all the remaining ingredients and fry for 10 minutes, mixing and stirring as you go, until everything starts to smell and look amazing. Season to taste with salt and pepper.

Transfer the cauliflower to the oven (either in the original frying pan if it's ovenproof, or in a baking dish) and roast for 30 minutes, or until charred and sweet, crunchy and soft – one truly delightful vegetable.

3 TABLESPOONS OLIVE OIL

1 WHOLE HEAD OF CAULIFLOWER, CUT INTO BITE-SIZED PIECES, INCLUDING THE STEM AND INNER LEAVES

1 TABLESPOON SWEET PAPRIKA

1 TABLESPOON GROUND TURMERIC

1 TABLESPOON SUMAC

ZEST AND JUICE OF 1 LEMON

SALT AND PEPPER

TIPS

1. Cookbooks often suggest steaming or boiling the cauliflower first to speed up the cooking but I find this significantly compromises the yumminess of the vegetable and would not recommend it.

2. If you're in a hurry you can eat the cauliflower after the initial frying – it just won't be as soft and luxurious as it is after roasting.

3. For a change of flavour, try using coconut oil instead of olive oil.

ROCK-BOTTOM MACARONI CHEESE

Sometimes I feel like I've hit rock-bottom when all I can cook for dinner is macaroni cheese. And yet ... everyone loves it. So maybe rock-bottom is where I belong? Traditional mac 'n' cheese recipes use white sauce, which you make on the stove top with butter and flour and milk, stirring for ages in a pan that you later have to wash. It's a major drag. Sour cream replaces the need for this and tastes perfect.

If you're desperate, skip the crumbs and the baking and just serve this up after the bit that says 'Season to taste with salt and pepper'. Spring onion greens also work well if you don't have any herbs. Serves 6

Cooking time: 20–25 minutes | Prep time: 5 minutes

Preheat the grill (broiler) to high or the oven to 180°C (350°F). Line a 25 cm × 32 cm (10 in × 13 in) ovenproof dish with baking paper.

Add the pasta to a large saucepan of boiling water and cook according to the packet instructions minus 2 minutes. Drain the pasta well and return it to the empty saucepan.

Add the sour cream, herbs and a third of the cheese to the pan and toss together well. Season to taste with salt and pepper.

Tip everything into the prepared dish and top with the rest of the cheese, followed by the breadcrumbs, then transfer to the oven and cook for 15 minutes or until golden on top. Serve with a raw salad of sugar-snap peas, cherry tomatoes and cucumber slices.

TIPS

1. If you want to turn this into a tuna bake, add a medium-sized tin of tuna (about 185 g/6½ oz) at the same time as the herbs. (My mum used to then top this with corn flakes instead of panko, which, as a child, both sickened and delighted me.)

2. If you buy grated cheese, I recommend you keep it in the freezer – it lasts much longer and still works fine in this recipe even if it hasn't been defrosted.

3. Fancy restaurants now serve mac 'n' cheese as a nostalgic retro dish. (I once paid $30 for one! To be honest, it was pretty great.) To take your mac 'n' cheese to the next level, use a combination of pecorino (65 g/2¼ oz), blue (90 g/3 oz) and mozzarella (225 g/8 oz) in place of the regular cheddar.

500 G (1 LB 2 OZ) MACARONI

300 G (10½ OZ) SOUR CREAM

LARGE HANDFUL OF PARSLEY OR BASIL, CHOPPED

375 G (13 OZ/3 CUPS) GRATED CHEDDAR

SALT AND PEPPER

60 G (2 OZ/1 CUP) PANKO BREADCRUMBS

TO SERVE

SUGAR-SNAP PEAS

CHERRY TOMATOES, HALVED

CUCUMBER, SLICED

RIGATONI CARBONARA

Overcooked pasta is gross. Avoid making your loved ones eat glue-like food by reading the cooking instructions on the packet and then subtracting a minute or two. It will continue to cook after the sauce has been stirred through. Serves 5

Cooking time: 15–20 minutes | Prep time: 10 minutes

Beat the egg in a bowl or jug, add the sour cream and cheese and mix together well. Set aside.

Warm a large, heavy-based frying pan over a low heat. Add the butter and, when frothing, add the bacon and leek and fry for 10 minutes, stirring occasionally. (It should be bubbling and smelling good at this point with the leek looking translucent and softened and the bacon cooked and yummy but not going like the blazes.)

Meanwhile, add the pasta to a large saucepan of boiling water and cook according to the packet instructions. When the pasta has only 3 minutes left to cook, add the peas, if using, to the frying pan with the bacon.

When the pasta is 1 minute from 'cooked', drain it well then add it to the frying pan. Turn off the heat, pour in the sour cream and egg mixture and stir it through quickly to mix everything together well. Serve immediately, topped with a few pieces of lovely raw tomato and a sprinkling of chilli flakes, if you like.

1 EGG

300 G (10½ OZ) SOUR CREAM

100 G (3½ OZ) PARMESAN OR GRANA PADANO, FINELY GRATED, PLUS EXTRA TO SERVE

70 G (2½ OZ) BUTTER

200 G (7 OZ) BEST-QUALITY BACON RASHERS (SLICES) CUT INTO 1 CM (½ IN) PIECES

1 LEEK, FINELY SLICED, OR 4 SPRING ONIONS (SCALLIONS), CUT INTO BATONS

500 G (1 LB 2 OZ) RIGATONI

80 G (2¾ OZ/½ CUP) FROZEN PEAS (OPTIONAL)

1 TOMATO, CHOPPED INTO BIG CHUNKS (OPTIONAL)

PINCH OF CHILLI FLAKES (OPTIONAL)

TIPS

1. Bacon is the real star here, so experiment with different smokehouses – the quality and taste varies wildly and makes a noticeable difference to this dish.

2. If you have some truffles that you've been saving (partly because they're so expensive and partly because you don't actually know what to do with them), then use a microplane to shave them over the carbonara just before serving.

AGEDASHI TOFU

I honestly thought this dish was too hard for a humble home cook like me! It's not. Remember, just because something is yummy does not mean it's impossible. Serves 4–6

Cooking time: 10 minutes | Prep time: 10 minutes

To make the sauce, add all the ingredients to a small saucepan, bring to a simmer over a medium heat and cook for 7 minutes, or until reduced by a third.

Remove the tofu from its packaging, dry it on a clean tea towel (dish towel) and use a sharp knife to cut it into roughly 4 cm x 4 cm (1½ in x 1½ in) squares.

Dust each tofu square generously in the flour, even giving it a second dusting if it looks like it's becoming wet again.

Fill a large saucepan with the oil and put it over a high heat. Check it is hot enough by dipping the handle of a wooden spoon into the oil – if the handle bubbles immediately, it's ready. Gently lower the tofu pieces into the hot oil and fry for 4 minutes, then turn and fry for another 4 minutes on the other side.

To serve, divide the cooked tofu cubes among serving bowls and top with a teeny tiny blob of grated ginger and a sprinkle of nori seaweed, if you like. Pour the sauce around the base of the tofu and serve.

500 G (1 LB 2 OZ) SILKEN TOFU

225 G (8 OZ/1½ CUPS) TAPIOCA FLOUR OR POTATO FLOUR

500 ML (17 FL OZ/2 CUPS) CANOLA OIL

SAUCE

250 ML (8½ FL OZ/1 CUP) DASHI STOCK

2 TABLESPOONS MIRIN

2 TABLESPOONS JAPANESE SOY SAUCE

TO SERVE (OPTIONAL)

1 x 2 CM (1 IN) PIECE FRESH GINGER, FINELY GRATED

1 NORI SEAWEED SHEET, CUT INTO MATCHSTICKS

TIPS

1. Tapioca flour and potato flour are common and cheap but are sometimes found hiding in either the Asian section of the supermarket or near the gravy ingredients. They can be substituted with cornflour (cornstarch) for 90 per cent yumminess.

2. I often skip making the sauce and just serve this with diluted soba sauce (see page 18) or bottled udon sauce.

'I WANT MORE' BRUSSELS SPROUTS

Let's be honest, a lot of things from childhood are genuinely horrendous – getting caught in a rip, eating clag, school. For me, brussels sprouts were fucking gross. A cruel and unusual torture and I couldn't understand why anyone would inflict them on an innocent and cute little person like me. They tasted like ... a vindictive maths teacher's glare. That was when my mum cooked them. Then I learned to cook them the way they're meant to be cooked. To maximise the flavour, cook out the bitterness and add sweetness and char. Try them this way and you'll be eating them for the rest of your life. *Serves 6 as a side*

Cooking time: 35–40 minutes | Prep time: 5 minutes

Preheat the oven to 180°C (350°F).

Melt the coconut oil in a large, heavy-based ovenproof frying pan over a medium–high heat. When sizzling hot, tip in the sprouts, cut side down, and fry for 15–20 minutes, turning halfway through cooking.

Pour over the maple syrup and give everything a good stir to coat all the sprouts as best you can – they should be looking charred and even a little black in places and giving off a nutty, sweet smell that makes people wander into the kitchen with expectant eyes. Transfer the pan to the oven and cook for a final 15–20 minutes. Spoon into a serving bowl, season to taste with salt and serve sprinkled with a handful of toasted slivered almonds, if you like.

4 TABLESPOONS COCONUT OIL OR BUTTER

650 G (1 LB 7 OZ) BRUSSELS SPROUTS, WOODY TIPS TRIMMED, HALVED

60 ML (2 FL OZ/¼ CUP) MAPLE SYRUP

SALT

LIGHTLY TOASTED SLIVERED ALMONDS, TO SERVE (OPTIONAL)

TIPS

1. Butter will burn quicker than coconut oil so reduce the cooking time to 7 minutes per side here, if using.

2. If you don't have an ovenproof frying pan, just tip everything into a baking tray after the initial frying and continue to cook as before.

3. Some people believe that sprouts make you fart. While this seems to be true if they're partially cooked, if you're cooking them to well-done like this then it isn't such a problem. And if you do happen to fart a bit, well, they're only airy, inoffensive farts – like what a fairy on a trampoline might do.

BASICALLY BEAUTIFUL ROAST POTATOES

I know this is basic, but every time people come over they want to know the secret of my roast potatoes. IT'S NOT A SECRET! This recipe is a simple method for achieving spuddy goodness. And no, I don't pre-salt or peel my potatoes because they don't need it. (Save the salt for after they're cooked to get the most bang out of your sprinkle.) Serves 4–6 as a side

Cooking time: 55 minutes–1 hour 5 minutes | Prep time: 5 minutes

Preheat the oven to 180°C (350°F). Prepare two baking trays by lining them with baking paper and adding half of the oil and butter to each.

Put all the potatoes in a large saucepan, cover with cold water and add the salt. Bring to the boil and cook for 5 minutes, then drain in a colander. Wearing rubber gloves, cut each hot potato into 4–6 pieces.

Meanwhile, pop the trays into the hot oven and leave for at least 5 minutes to get the butter and oil mixture thoroughly hot. Remove from the oven and toss the potato pieces through the hot butter and oil mixture, trying to arrange the pieces on the tray cut side down.

Roast for 50 minutes, turning the potatoes onto their other cut-side faces halfway through cooking. If the colour is looking good at this point you can serve the potatoes like this, otherwise turn the potato pieces onto their skin sides and give them a final 10 minutes. Pile into a large bowl and serve immediately.

80 ML (2½ FL OZ/⅓ CUP) OLIVE OIL

80 G (2¾ OZ) BUTTER

1.5 KG (3 LB 5 OZ) ALL-PURPOSE POTATOES

1 TEASPOON SALT

RICH PERSON'S ROASTED VEG

Let me try to describe the feeling I get when I sit down to a plate of delicious roasted Jerusalem artichokes ... warmth suffuses my body, my eyes shine/water a bit and my heart feels as though it might burst with gladness! Vegetables – when cooked well and served in generous quantities – make me feel like the richest person in the world, and roasted vegetables are one of the greatest foods ever invented. This is a painless way to get the most flavour out of some of the fanciest ones. Serves 6 as a side

Cooking time: 45–50 minutes | Prep time: 10 minutes

Preheat the oven to 180°C (350°F). Line your largest roasting tin with baking paper.

Arrange the vegetables on the tray in a single layer, then pour over the melted butter and toss to coat (if they look too crowded, set up a second roasting tin). Roast for 30 minutes, give everything a turn, then roast for a final 15–20 minutes until the artichokes look golden and lightly caramelised. Serve as an accompaniment to a roast chicken or 'Sets of 10' Barbecued Eye Fillet (page 98), or alongside my Greenest Salad and Tiny Cheese Pies (pages 104 and 118).

1 KG (2 LB 3 OZ) JERUSALEM ARTICHOKES, HALVED LENGTHWAYS

1 BUNCH BABY CARROTS, STRINGY BITS TRIMMED

2 RED ONIONS, PEELED AND CUT INTO WEDGES

115 G (4 OZ) BUTTER, MELTED

TIPS

1. Keep an eye on market prices for Jerusalem artichokes. Sometimes they're crazy expensive but when you get them midseason, they cost the same per weight as sweet potato.

2. Add parsnips or teeny beetroot (beets) here if you love 'em.

MISO SOUP WITH PIPIS

There's a trick to miso soup that you need to know: once the miso paste is added to the broth you must not boil it, as to do so irrevocably alters its delicate flavour. My mum has a cheat when she makes miso soup – she uses an instant miso sachet along with the regular ingredients. Inside the miso sachet you get dried green onion, seaweed, dashi flavour and a few other ingredients, which help to plump up the complexity of the soup's flavour. Serves 6

Cooking time: 15 minutes | Prep time: 10 minutes

Soak the wakame seaweed in a bowl of cold water for 2 minutes, then drain and chop.

Bring the water to the boil in a saucepan, add the pipis, soaked wakame seaweed and instant miso sachet, if using, and cook until the pipis have opened, about 3 minutes.

Reduce the heat to very low and add the silken tofu. Spoon a ladleful of the hot broth into a small bowl or jug and stir in the miso paste to dissolve, then return it to the pan along with the chopped spring onion. Give everything a gentle stir (being careful not to scramble the tofu), taste the soup and add a little more water if it's too salty. Divide among small bowls and serve.

1 TABLESPOON WAKAME SEAWEED

1 LITRE (34 FL OZ/4 CUPS) COLD WATER, PLUS EXTRA IF NECESSARY

100 G (3½ OZ) PIPIS OR CLAMS (VONGOLE)

1 × INSTANT MISO SACHET (OPTIONAL)

100 G (3½ OZ) SILKEN TOFU, CUT INTO 5 MM (¼ IN) CUBES

2 TABLESPOONS WHITE MISO PASTE

40 G (1½ OZ/⅓ CUP) CHOPPED SPRING ONION (SCALLION)

TIPS

1. I have a special love of eating tiny clams because the kids can find them at the beach and feel a particular pride when their catch gets eaten, even if it's just one per bowl. However, in some areas eating pipis from the beach is not recommended, particularly after rainfall, so make sure you know what you've found is safe and legal to eat!

2. This soup is easy to make vegan – just leave out the pipis.

IDIOT-PROOF SALMON

If you cook this right, the skin will be crispy and delicious and it's worth nailing because fish skin is packed with goodness. Salmon is great entry-level seafood – it's available at most supermarkets, kids will eat it and, with this recipe, it's pretty much impossible to fuck up. Choose fillets with glossy, firm flesh and the skin left on.

I've written this for 4 people, but apply common sense – it's one fillet per person and is easy to adjust for the number of mouths you're feeding. Serves 4

Cooking time: 10 minutes | Prep time: 5 minutes

In a large bowl, season the salmon fillets with salt and pepper (go easy on the salt – you can always add more but you can't take it away), then sprinkle all over with the sesame seeds. Add the flour and give everything a mix around to coat lightly on all sides.

Melt the coconut oil in a non-stick frying pan over a medium heat (don't allow the pan to get too hot – it's not a blasting you want here). Add the salmon to the pan, skin side down, and fry for 5 minutes, then turn and cook for a further 4 minutes, or until looking golden and feeling firm.

Divide the salmon fillets among plates and serve with rice, avocado slices, seaweed, lemon wedges and an umeboshi plum, if you like, along with a blob of mayo and a shallow dish of soy sauce on the side.

TIP

If you're interested in gut health, the Japanese umeboshi plum is brilliant. Treat them like an extremely intense condiment. They are sour and salty and – as with wasabi – you only need a microscopic amount to go on each mouthful. In a typical Japanese meal, one small plum is enough for one adult.

4 × 150 G (5½ OZ) SALMON FILLETS, SKIN ON

SALT AND PEPPER

40 G (1½ OZ/¼ CUP) SESAME SEEDS

50 G (1¾ OZ/⅓ CUP) PLAIN (ALL-PURPOSE) FLOUR

3 TABLESPOONS COCONUT OIL

TO SERVE

ABSORPTION-METHOD COOKED RICE (SEE PAGE 13)

FIRM, RIPE AVOCADOS, CUT INTO WEDGES

NORI SEAWEED SHEETS, CUT INTO STRIPS

LEMON WEDGES

UMEBOSHI PLUM (OPTIONAL)

KEWPIE MAYONNAISE

JAPANESE SOY SAUCE

SAN CHOI BAO

When I was a kid my parents used to take us to the most upmarket restaurant in the world (or so we thought). It was the local Chinese and the waiters brought us these beauties every time. We called them 'Chinese hamburgers' and thought they were the single greatest invention in the history of food. This recipe here is mind-blowingly easy, though there is some chopping involved – make sure everything is prepped and ready to go but kept in separate piles before you start cooking. And please do as you're told and follow the recipe even though it probably seems too easy and simple to be good. It works. Serves 6

Cooking time: 10 minutes | Prep time: 20 minutes

Set a wok over a very high heat. Add the oils and red onion and stir-fry for 2 minutes, then add the pork, garlic and ginger and continue to stir-fry for 4 minutes, or until the pork is almost cooked.

Add the carrot to the wok and cook for 2–3 minutes, then add the zucchini, mushroom, asparagus, capsicum, oyster sauce, spring onion and water chestnuts one at a time and leaving 1–2 minutes between each, stirring all the while as you go, until all the ingredients have been added and are cooked.

Place the wok on a heatproof surface in the middle of the table and serve immediately with the lettuce cups in a serving bowl. To eat, everyone grabs a lettuce leaf and stuffs it with the meat filling. Chilli fans can add their own fresh chilli or spoonful of sambal oelek. Wrap up and enjoy!

TIPS

1. It may be tempting to add more ginger than this to the recipe, but if you're cooking for children, I suggest you don't. Tread lightly here ...

2. If asparagus is not in season then replace it with your choice of green beans, snow peas (mangetout) or shelled edamame. Minced chicken in place of the pork works here too, though it's not quite so tasty.

3. Water chestnuts are available from all mainstream supermarkets and can often be found in the Asian section. They are unique for staying crunchy even when cooked (and tinned) and are not actually nuts at all but are, in fact, aquatic vegetables! If you're avoiding carbs, leave them out of this recipe.

1 TABLESPOON SESAME OIL

2 TABLESPOONS PEANUT, CANOLA OR RICE BRAN OIL

1 SMALL RED ONION, DICED

600 G (1 LB 5 OZ) MINCED (GROUND) PORK

1 GARLIC CLOVE, FINELY GRATED OR MINCED

1 CM (½ IN) PIECE FRESH GINGER, FINELY GRATED

1 CARROT, FINELY CHOPPED

1 ZUCCHINI (COURGETTE), GRATED

200 G (7 OZ) MUSHROOMS, DICED

1 BUNCH OF ASPARAGUS, FINELY CHOPPED

½ RED CAPSICUM (BELL PEPPER), DICED

3 TABLESPOONS OYSTER SAUCE

6 SPRING ONIONS (SCALLIONS), FINELY CHOPPED

110 G (4 OZ) TINNED SLICED WATER CHESTNUTS, CHOPPED

1 ICEBERG LETTUCE, CUT INTO CUPS

CHOPPED FRESH CHILLI OR A JAR OF SAMBAL OELEK, TO SERVE (OPTIONAL)

YUMI'S FAMOUS CHICKEN WINGS (A.K.A. 'THE VEGETARIAN CONVERTERS')

If you're only going to cook one recipe from this cookbook, please make it this one. These wings sum up exactly what I'm going for here – they are something legitimately yummy, they're easy to make and they will impress and delight those you love. This is a recipe handed down by my mum and it's famous for converting one of my long-term vegetarian friends, Julie, back to meat after twenty years, hence the nickname.

There are a few tricks to making this chicken perfect. 1. I always trim off the third joint of the wing because (a) I don't like it and (b) it is often the first part to burn, stinking out your house. 2. Avoid trying to cook this recipe too hot and fast, or the results will not be as delicious. Wait it out, give the sauce time to get really sticky and coat the chicken. Making the marinade is a bit time-consuming so I make up a big batch and save the rest for another time – it stores in a glass jar in the fridge for months. Serves 6

Cooking time: 1 hour 20 minutes | Prep time: 10 minutes

Preheat the oven to 175°C (345°F). Have an oven rack on the middle shelf of the oven and line two high-sided baking trays with foil first, then baking paper.

To make the marinade, put all the ingredients in a food processor and blend together for 2 minutes.

Cram the chicken pieces onto the prepared baking trays, skin side down, in a single layer. Spoon a quarter to a third of the marinade over the chicken to coat generously (store the rest in a glass jar in the fridge with the lid tightly screwed on for next time).

Bake for 30 minutes, then turn the pieces over with tongs and bake for another 20 minutes. Turn the chicken again and bake for a final 15 minutes, turning the chicken one last time halfway through cooking to get maximum sauce coverage.

2.5 KG (5½ LB) CHICKEN WINGS, THIRD JOINT REMOVED

MARINADE

2 GARLIC BULBS, PEELED AND TRIMMED

8 CM (3¼ IN) PIECE FRESH GINGER, ROUGHLY CHOPPED

2 LONG RED CHILLIES, DESEEDED

500 G (1 LB 2 OZ) HONEY

500 ML (17 FL OZ/2 CUPS) JAPANESE SOY SAUCE

TIPS

1. These wings are unreal cold – I always make extra and put them into zip-lock bags for weekday lunches or take them to non-cook friends and use them as bribes (I once swapped a batch of these for a brand-new double bed, no kidding).

2. It's important to use Japanese soy sauce here as the character of the sauce varies greatly depending on country of origin.

I'M IN A HURRY ROAST CHICKEN

Okay, for this recipe you still need time, but that's for the cooking. The preparation takes only a couple of minutes. My local butcher (who is notable for being female in a male-dominated business) suggested I try cooking chicken like this in 2011 and I have never looked back. Serves 4–6

Cooking time: 1 hour–1 hour 10 minutes | Prep time: 5 minutes

Preheat the oven to 180°C (350°F).

Tip all the potatoes into a small, heavy-based roasting tin. Place the chicken on top.

Pour the oil over the chicken and massage it in with your fingers, then season generously with salt and pepper and sprinkle over 1 teaspoon each of the paprika and sumac. Transfer to the oven and set a timer on your phone for 30 minutes.

Once your 30 minutes are up, use tongs to turn the chook. (If you can be bothered, you can turn the spuds as well though it doesn't matter if you don't – it just evens out the colour.) Season generously again with salt and pepper and sprinkle over the remaining spices, then roast for a further 30 minutes. Check your chicken's cooked by driving a skewer into its fattest part – if the juices run clear, it's good to eat. If it isn't or the chicken doesn't look brown enough at this point, set your oven grill (broiler) to high and leave it in for another 7–10 minutes.

Cut the chicken up and don't be afraid to use scissors – I find it easier. Serve with the potatoes, something green and something red (e.g. sugar-snap peas and cherry tomatoes).

1 KG (2 LB 3 OZ) NEW POTATOES

1 × 1.5 KG (3 LB 5 OZ) CHICKEN

2 TABLESPOONS OLIVE OIL

SALT AND PEPPER

2 TEASPOONS SWEET PAPRIKA

2 TEASPOONS SUMAC

TO SERVE

SUGAR-SNAP PEAS

CHERRY TOMATOES

TIPS

1. If you want to get fancy, try stuffing the chicken cavity with a small lemon that you've pricked with a fork along with some fresh herbs and/or some whole garlic cloves.

2. A few years ago a friend who has three kids said to me, 'I think we've become a two-chook family!' I knew exactly what she meant. Sometimes you accidentally have so many children that one chicken isn't enough. If that's you, add an extra chicken. In a good oven the cooking times don't change here but it'll be harder to get the colour right, so work the top element of your grill and be generous with the spices.

ZERO F*CKS SNACKS, EMERGENCIES & OTHER MOMENTS OF DESPERATION

What happens when people arrive suddenly for late-night crisis talks or an impromptu kid gathering and everyone is starving but you have absolutely nothing prepared? Everything in this section is designed to use ingredients you probably have lying around. None of it is meant to be impressive. And if even *these* recipes seem too hard, I think you might have earned yourself some takeaway. FYI, I always keep a good loaf of sliced bread in the freezer, because you just never know...

ANCHOVY TOAST

My brother-in-law loves anchovies and every Christmas I try to find him a different tin from some far-flung place. Sometimes they cost, like, $40. This clearly makes me an unusually awesome non-blood relative. I never get to find out if they're any good myself because they live interstate. Ripped off. This recipe goes great with beer and you don't even have to use $40 anchovies. (Though it helps if you like anchovies.) Serves 4

Cooking time: 5 minutes | Prep time: 5 minutes

Preheat the grill (broiler) to high and arrange the bread on a baking tray.

Lay 6 anchovies out onto a slice of bread at an angle, leaving a 1 cm (½ in) gap between each. Repeat with the rest of the anchovies and bread slices.

Place under the grill and cook until the bread is just going golden, about 3 minutes.

Serve immediately with frosty cold drinks.

4 SLICES BEST-QUALITY SOURDOUGH BREAD, PREFERABLY WITH A SESAME SEED CRUST

24 TINNED OR JARRED ANCHOVIES

TIPS

1. This might be using up a spare fuck you don't have, but if you want to take this snack to the next level, garnish it with a shake of hot cayenne pepper and a sprinkle of sweet paprika or shichimi togarashi.

2. If your bread is a bit stale, butter it first, but still only grill one side.

POACHED EGGS

It wasn't until I worked in a very busy breakfast restaurant kitchen that I understood the cult that surrounds poached eggs – people honestly think they are a luxury food that they have to pay a fancy chef to make for them. Not so, you just have to be a cool cat. Don't stress out. It's easy, it just looks hard. And use fresh eggs. Serves as many as you want

Cooking time: 5 minutes | Prep time: 5 minutes

Half-fill a small, non-stick saucepan with 750 ml (25½ fl oz/ 3 cups) water and bring to the boil. Add the vinegar and lower the heat so that the water is at a low simmer.

Working slowly one egg at a time, crack the eggs and then gently lower them into the water, leaving space between each and waiting for the water to get hot again before adding another. (If you are nervous about cracking the eggs directly into the pot, crack each one first into a small bowl, then tip it into the boiling water – any eggs with broken yolks can be set aside and repurposed.)

Cook the eggs for 3 minutes without stirring, then scoop an egg out of the pan with a slotted spoon and inspect – if there's still a bit of gelatinous goo near the yolk it can go back in the boiling water for another 30 seconds or so. When cooked, drain your eggs on a clean tea towel (dish towel), then serve on toast with some sliced avocado and tomato, a few rocket leaves, a shaving or two of good cheese and a sprinkle of cracked black pepper.

60 ML (2 FL OZ/¼ CUP) WHITE VINEGAR

FRESH RAW EGGS

TO SERVE

YOUR BEST SOURDOUGH TOAST

AVOCADO, HALVED AND SLICED

TOMATOES, THE YUMMIEST YOU CAN FIND, SLICED

ROCKET (ARUGULA)

GOOD HARD CHEESE (E.G. PECORINO OR AGED CHEDDAR), SLICED AS THINLY AS POSSIBLE

CRACKED BLACK PEPPER

TIPS

1. If your eggs keep breaking and the yolk leaks out when you're making these then it is very likely that the eggs are not fresh. This is not your fault! Buy some more and try again.

2. Even when poaching for a large group of people I still like to use a fairly small-to-medium pan and cook the eggs in batches. I think it's easier to manage and the cooking eggs keep pace with the toaster's capabilities.

GOOGY AND RICE

This was the ultimate comfort food for my sisters, brother and me when we were little. 'Googy' was our baby word for egg, and this is what my mum would make when we were sick, as a treat when my dad was away, or just when we had some precious one-on-one time with her. It's the easiest thing in the world to put together, and it works just as well with reheated rice.

Now that I have kids of my own this is what they eat whenever I'm desperate, which is nearly every day... Serves 2

Cooking time: 10 minutes | Prep time: 2 minutes

Use a fork to beat the egg together with the soy sauce in a small cup or jug.

While the rice is as hot as it can be (but off the stove) pour the egg over it and very gently mix it through with a rice spoon or chopsticks.

Serve in individual bowls topped with a sprinkling of seaweed ribbons, if you like.

1 EGG

1 TABLESPOON JAPANESE SOY SAUCE

550 G (1 LB 3 OZ/3 CUPS) ABSORPTION-METHOD COOKED RICE (SEE PAGE 13), STEAMING HOT

1 NORI SEAWEED SHEET, CUT INTO RIBBONS (OPTIONAL)

TIP

This is easy to change up. Add daikon (white radish) pickle, umeboshi plum or natto if you're a bit Japanese, avocado or smoked salmon if you're feeling fancy or perhaps just some simple tinned tuna.

CHICKEN YAKITORI

When you duck down through the door of a bar in Japan and an unmistakeable smoky, burnt barbecue smell hits you, you know you're in the right place. You should be smelling that same smell with this brilliantly simple dish. Asian grocers sell pre-made yakitori sauces – I have experimented with several of these and have found them all to be fine! If you can, make life easier for yourself and use a pre-bought sauce. Serves 4–6

Cooking time: 15 minutes | Prep time: 10 minutes

If making the sauce, mix all the ingredients together in a small saucepan over a medium heat, bring to a simmer and cook for 5 minutes, or until reduced by half. Set aside.

Turn the barbecue up to high.

Thread the chicken and spring onion pieces alternately onto bamboo skewers. Brush the skewers lightly with oil, then place on the chargrill plate and cook for 4 minutes on each side. (The exact cooking time will vary depending on your barbecue – you want them to be pretty cooked at this point but not 'done' as there is still another 4 minutes of cooking to go.)

Brush the skewers with the yakitori sauce and continue to cook for 4 minutes, turning and brushing as you go, until you have coated each side 3–4 times. Everything should sizzle and smoke, go a little charred and smell utterly tantalising. Serve immediately with rice and plenty of Japanese beer.

TIPS

1. If you want to try this without using the barbecue, it's common to cook yakitori under a hot, high grill (broiler). It won't have quite the same smell but it'll still be cool. Arrange the skewers on a tray and set it 8 cm (3¼ in) away from the top element of the preheated grill. Give it 6 minutes before brushing the skewers with the sauce and turning every minute for 3–4 minutes.

2. In Japan you can get all kinds of different cuts of chicken for this dish. A thigh cut would generally have the skin on, which gives a fattier, more moist and indulgent result. If you make this dish regularly, I'd strongly recommend you try it with skin-on meat. If you can't find thigh fillets with the skin on, use skin-on thigh 'cutlets' and just cut the bone out.

3. This sauce is also great on fish fillets – cover them generously in it before putting them on a lined baking tray and popping them under a nice, hot grill for 7 minutes until cooked.

4. A lot of recipes tell you to soak skewers in water to prevent them from burning. I never do this. Most of the time they don't burn, sometimes they do – it doesn't bother me.

100 ML (3½ FL OZ) YAKITORI SAUCE (SHOP-BOUGHT OR HOME-MADE, SEE BELOW)

8 BONELESS CHICKEN THIGHS, SKIN ON AND CUT INTO 2 CM (¾ IN) PIECES

8 SPRING ONIONS (SCALLIONS), TRIMMED AND CUT INTO 2 CM (¾ IN) BATONS

PEANUT OIL (OR OTHER FLAVOURLESS OIL SUCH AS CANOLA OR GRAPESEED), FOR BRUSHING

ABSORPTION-METHOD COOKED RICE (SEE PAGE 13), TO SERVE

YAKITORI SAUCE

50 ML (1¾ FL OZ) JAPANESE SOY SAUCE

60 ML (2 FL OZ/¼ CUP) SAKÈ

70 ML (2¼ FL OZ) MIRIN

2 TEASPOONS CASTER SUGAR

1 TABLESPOON SOFT BROWN SUGAR

BARBECUED LAMB CUTLETS

Lamb cutlets are pretty much the most expensive protein that my kids love. They feel and taste like a treat and the meat itself has an amazing flavour that needs zero fussing. I like them because they're naturally lean and take only moments to cook. The trick with cutlets is not to overcook them – you want them nice and pink. Serves 4

Cooking time: 5 minutes | Prep time: 5 minutes

Thirty minutes before cooking, take the cutlets out of the fridge and put them in a bowl together with the lemon zest, garlic and rosemary, if using. Toss together well to coat evenly and set aside to reach room temperature.

Get the hotplate of your barbecue stinkingly hot and have the rest of what you're planning to eat pretty much close to plated and ready to go (broccoli or salad, plus potatoes would be my recommendation).

If the cutlets have a fatty rind, start by using tongs to hold them against the barbecue hotplate, rind side down, until the fat has browned, then lay the cutlets down and cook for no more than 2 minutes on each side, sprinkling them with a little salt as they cook. Plate up immediately and enjoy.

12 LAMB CUTLETS

ZEST OF 1 LEMON

2 TABLESPOONS WHIPPED GARLIC OR 2 VERY FINELY CHOPPED GARLIC CLOVES

1 TABLESPOON FINELY CHOPPED ROSEMARY (OPTIONAL)

SALT

TO SERVE

BROCCOLI FLORETS OR SALAD

POTATOES

TIP

Supermarket lamb cutlets tend to be thinner than the butcher-bought variety, so require less cooking time. If you've picked up the nice, thick butcher's ones then you might want to give them a little more time on each side but be careful – you really don't want to go 'well-done' on a lamb cutlet.

'SETS OF 10' BARBECUED EYE FILLET

This method simplifies the cooking of an entire eye fillet to four easy sets of 10 minutes, and it works every time. Have your phone or timer ready. The changing width of the fillet (all fillets taper in like a wind sock) means everyone at the barbecue can have a piece cooked to their liking: well-done at the skinny end, lovely and rare up the fat end.

Eye fillet steak always seemed like the ultimate rich-person's food to me when I was growing up. It was super, super special-occasion and one of my dad's favourite foods. Nowadays the price seems more commensurate with fancy snags or lamb chops – affordable enough to do at a special barbecue, but expensive enough to want to make sure you get it right. Luckily, this recipe is pretty hard to muck up – just be sure to choose a nice solid fillet, not one that's mangled at the thick end. Serves 6

Cooking time: 40 minutes | Prep time: 5 minutes

Take the meat out of the fridge at least one good hour before cooking. (It is worth setting an alarm on your phone to make sure this happens on time as it is a crucial step for getting the meat cooked perfectly.)

Preheat the barbecue to very hot.

In a clean bowl, drizzle olive oil over the fillet and season well with salt and pepper.

Lay the fillet out straight along the hottest part of the barbecue hotplate. Cook for 10 minutes, using tongs to turn the meat, to give it a gorgeous brown crust all over.

Lower the barbecue heat to medium–low, transfer the meat onto a metal baking tray and return it to the hotplate (creating a barrier between the meat and the heat), then close the lid and leave to cook for another 10 minutes.

Turn the meat over, add the sliced onions wherever the meat juices are pooling in the pan, then cook with the lid closed for a final 10 minutes.

Remove the meat to a clean serving plate, cover first with foil and then a clean tea towel (dish towel) and leave to rest for 10 minutes. (Don't be tempted to carve the meat before this time is up.) If the onions need a bit more cooking, pop them on the barbecue and turn off the heat.

To serve, set the fillet out on the table and carve it up into generous slices, retaining as much of the juice as you can, and enjoy the sound of everyone oohing and aahing.

1 × WHOLE BEEF EYE-FILLET (ABOUT 1.3–1.7 KG/2 LB 14 OZ–3 LB 12 OZ)

2 TABLESPOONS OLIVE OIL

SALT AND PEPPER

2 ONIONS, PEELED AND SLICED

TIPS

1. Be sure to swat away any interfering guests who want to turn the meat – it will slow the process and confuse the cook.

2. Experienced barbecuers will be able to tell whether the meat is cooked to their liking by prodding it firmly with a finger. (It springs back the more cooked it is.)

CHARGRILLED BROCCOLI SALAD

During my last two pregnancies I developed gestational diabetes, which meant I had to drastically overhaul my diet. I found it infuriating at times but one effect that has outlasted the pregnancies is a deep-rooted love for green vegetables, in particular, barbecued broccoli. I discovered this miracle in a recipe book called Community, which put salads front and centre and inspired its readers, myself included, to eat a lot more greenery. This salad counts that book as inspiration. Serves 6 with leftovers

Cooking time: 10 minutes | Prep time: 10 minutes

Preheat the barbecue to very hot.

In a large bowl and working with your hands to ensure the pieces are covered, toss the broccoli florets through the olive oil, lemon zest and lemon juice, then season generously with salt and pepper. Spread the broccoli over the barbecue hotplate and cook for 10 minutes, turning at 3–minute intervals, until charred all over. Don't be afraid of a little bit of blackness on the broccoli – these are the most delicious bits.

Add the spinach, feta and chickpeas to a serving bowl and mix everything together well, then tip in your cooked broccoli, drizzle over the macadamia oil, add a big squeeze of lemon and give everything a last toss. Serve.

850 G (1 LB 14 OZ) BROCCOLI FLORETS

3 TABLESPOONS OLIVE OIL

ZEST AND JUICE OF 1 LEMON, PLUS EXTRA LEMON JUICE TO SERVE

SALT AND PEPPER

100 G (3½ OZ/2 CUPS) BABY SPINACH

150 G (5½ OZ) FETA, CUBED

400 G (14 OZ) TINNED CHICKPEAS, DRAINED AND RINSED

1 TABLESPOON MACADAMIA OIL OR OLIVE OIL

THE GREENEST SALAD

'Renae and Ralph are doing the steak and Maxine is bringing her famous carrot cake, there's going to be a bunch of hungry people – do you reckon you could bring a big salad?' Yes, yes I could. Serves 8–12

Cooking time: 5 minutes | Prep time: 10 minutes

Blanch the edamame in a saucepan of boiling water for 5 minutes until tender. Drain and set aside to cool.

Wash the snow peas in a colander under a kettleful of boiling water, then rinse immediately in cold water until cold. Drain, then spread the peas on a dry tea towel (dish towel). Repeat this process with the green beans.

Pop the drained edamame, peas and beans in a big bowl together with the remaining salad ingredients.

To make the dressing, mix the ingredients together in a small bowl or shake them together in a tiny jar.

Pour the dressing over the salad, toss, taste and serve.

150 G (5½ OZ) SHELLED EDAMAME

600 G (1 LB 5 OZ) SNOW PEAS (MANGETOUT), TOPPED AND TAILED

600 G (1 LB 5 OZ) GREEN BEANS, TOPPED AND TAILED

100 G (3½ OZ/2 CUPS) BABY SPINACH LEAVES

1 BUNCH MINT, CHOPPED

140 G (5 OZ/1 CUP) TOASTED AND PEELED HAZELNUTS, LIGHTLY CHOPPED

DRESSING

ZEST AND JUICE OF 1 LEMON

2 TABLESPOONS MACADAMIA OIL

1 GARLIC CLOVE, FINELY GRATED

¼ TEASPOON SALT

1 TABLESPOON MAPLE SYRUP

TIP

Using the kettle to cook the beans is an idiot-proof way to make sure you don't overcook them. If you like your green beans cooked a little more, place them in a bowl (rather than a colander) before pouring over the boiling water and leave them to sit for 1 minute before draining and rinsing in cold water.

LIFE-GIVING SPICY CASHEW DIP

This dip, or sauce, or whatever you want to call it, is so yummy it gives life. Try it with crusty bread or pitta chips or make it your go-to for burgers, falafel or tofu steaks. Serves 8

Cooking time: 10 minutes | Prep time: 5 minutes

Add the cashews, sesame seeds, cumin and chilli to a dry frying pan set over a medium heat and toast, stirring, until the mix is fragrant and the sesame seeds are starting to go golden, about 3–4 minutes. Tip the mixture into a food processor then return the pan to the heat, adding the oil.

Add the garlic and the tomatoes to the pan and cook until the tomatoes collapse, about 5 minutes. Transfer to the food processor with the cashew mixture, add the salt and sugar and process until smooth.

Serve warm or chilled. Any leftover dip can be stored in an airtight container in the fridge for up to 10 days.

150 G (5½ OZ) CASHEWS

2 TABLESPOONS SESAME SEEDS

1 TEASPOON GROUND CUMIN

1 TEASPOON MILD CHILLI FLAKES

1 TABLESPOON OLIVE OIL

1 GARLIC CLOVE, CRUSHED

500 G (1 LB 2 OZ) TOMATOES, CHOPPED

¼ TEASPOON SALT

1 TABLESPOON SOFT BROWN SUGAR

TIP

The chilli heat tends to cool down as this dip sits, so if you want it to be extra spicy, add more.

EDAMAME GUACAMOLE

There is something magically creamy about this dip! I love adding it to a ploughman's lunch – we'll lay it out as part of a spread of the best bread rolls, the nicest ham, a few slices of amazing cheese and some locally made butter and ripe tomatoes. And if my daughter's friends end up hanging out in the evening and they want to clutter up the lounge room with their stinky teenage bodies watching telly and talking utter nonsense, I'll treat them to the leftovers with corn chips, carrot sticks and a free lecture about how music was better in my day. Serves 6

Cooking time: none | Prep time: 5 minutes

Put everything in the food processor and blend together until smooth. Pile into a bowl and serve with tortilla chips and veg sticks or as part of a ploughman's lunch. The dip will keep, covered in plastic wrap in the fridge, for up to 12 hours.

400 G (14 OZ) AVOCADO FLESH (ABOUT 3–4 AVOCADOS)

150 G (5½ OZ) SHELLED EDAMAME

JUICE OF 1–2 LIMES

1 BUNCH CORIANDER (CILANTRO) LEAVES

30 G (1 OZ/½ CUP) SPRING ONIONS (SCALLIONS), GREEN TOPS ONLY, SLICED

½ TEASPOON SALT

TO SERVE (OPTIONAL)

TORTILLA CHIPS

VEG STICKS

TIPS

1. For a chunkier texture, blend everything except the avocado and spring onions. Finely chop the spring onions and mash the avocados with a fork before adding to the blended combo, mixing well.

2. You can buy edamame already shelled from the Asian grocer and many mainstream green-grocers. Look carefully for them as the packaging is almost identical to the packaging for regular edamame in their pods.

ZERO
F*CKS
WEEKENDS

I love it when the family can eat together on weekends and often put on a big spread that will accommodate blow-ins, the kids' friends and of course the odd tricky eater. My favourite is when I'm organised and have prepared something in advance, so when the moment of sharing arrives, I don't miss out.

BRUSCHETTA SALAD

Recently we had friends over for lunch who were preparing to take an overseas flight that afternoon. Knowing they were going to be stuck for many hours eating processed plane food, I made this salad. It is so good, so fresh, so full of zing. It tastes like life. Dan, my friend, was amazed and kept complimenting it. 'It's easy to make,' I said. 'I'll send you the recipe.' He sighed, 'Food never tastes like this when I make it.' I asked, 'Do you follow the recipe? Do you measure the ingredients?' 'No. I like to get creative,' he said. I said, 'FOLLOW THE DAMN RECIPE!' Serves 6–8

Cooking time: 15 minutes | Prep time: 10 minutes

Preheat the oven to 200°C (400°F) or a barbecue to high.

Put the onion in a small bowl, pour over the balsamic vinegar and sprinkle over a pinch of salt. Set aside until needed. (This lightly pickles the onion and neutralises its peppery kick.)

Put the bread chunks, 3 tablespoons of the olive oil and a pinch of salt in a large bowl and toss together well. Lightly squeeze the bread chunks with your hands to get the oil into them before spreading them out onto a chargrill plate or roasting tray and cooking for 15 minutes until charred and crispy. Remove from the heat and set aside to cool slightly.

In the same large bowl, toss together the tomatoes, basil, mint and parsley, then add the crunchy bread chunks and the onion together with the balsamic pickling liquid. Add the remaining olive oil, toss together thoroughly and season to taste. Serve.

½ SMALL RED ONION, FINELY SLICED

3 TABLESPOONS BEST-QUALITY BALSAMIC VINEGAR

2 PINCHES OF SALT

450 G (1 LB) SOURDOUGH BREAD, CUT INTO BITE-SIZED CHUNKS

100 ML (3½ FL OZ) BEST-QUALITY FRUITY AND LIGHT OLIVE OIL

750 G (1 LB 11 OZ) BEST-QUALITY MIXED TOMATOES, CUT INTO QUARTERS OR HALVES IF LARGE

1 BUNCH BASIL LEAVES

½ BUNCH MINT LEAVES

1 BUNCH FLAT-LEAF (ITALIAN) PARSLEY LEAVES

PEPPER

TIPS

1. I use a mix of tomatoes here in both size and type: cherry toms, grape tomatoes, heirloom, vine-ripened reds ... whatever looks good at the shops. And when you get them home, don't refrigerate your tomatoes. Ever. For some reason I didn't learn this until well into adulthood (they should teach it in school).

2. If you don't have any decent sourdough, a halved, toasted and chopped up bagel has the chewiness you're going for.

3. To take this to the next level, try adding some shavings of Grana Padano/parmesan.

'THE TRICK' POTATO BAKE

This is one of those dishes a person can become known for – no kidding, my ex misses this dish more than me. Anyway, it's really easy to put together but like most potato dishes, it can't be rushed. Leaving the potato slices to soak in boiling water before baking is genius because it gives them a head-start on the cooking so you're not stuck waiting around for ages for the middle to soften. We've all been there when someone's painfully slow spud bake looks all golden on top but is still raw and hard inside. Not on my watch, not with my trick. Serves 6

Cooking time: 45 minutes | Prep time: 15 minutes

Preheat the oven to 175°C (345°F). Fill the kettle right to the limit with water and get it on to boil.

Slice the potatoes on the thinnest setting of a mandoline. (A food processor's slicing setting will also work but your slices won't be as wonderfully thin.)

Transfer the potato slices to the largest bowl you own, sprinkle over the salt then pour over the boiling water straight from the kettle to cover. Wearing rubber gloves, give the potato slices a quick slosh in the water and spend a moment separating them so that they don't stick together. Set aside.

Fill up the kettle to the top again and put it on the boil again. Line a 23 × 30 cm (9 × 12 in) ovenproof dish with baking paper and give the paper a spray with oil.

Once the kettle has boiled, drain the potatoes in a colander, then return them to the bowl and pour over the freshly boiled water. Leave the potatoes to sit in the water for 4 minutes, then drain them very well and return them to the empty bowl. Add the sour cream and half the cheese, season lightly and toss together well to coat the potato slices evenly.

Tip the potato slices into the prepared dish. You don't need to arrange them neatly - it makes no difference and is a waste of time – but do spread them out evenly by feeling how they sit in the tray with your fingers and rearranging as necessary. Top with the remaining cheese, transfer to the oven and bake for at least 45 minutes, or until it's bubbling and looking golden and delicious on top.

2 KG (4 LB 6 OZ) ALL-PURPOSE POTATOES

1 TEASPOON SALT

OLIVE OIL SPRAY, FOR GREASING

300 G (10½ OZ) SOUR CREAM

250 G (9 OZ/2 CUPS) GRATED CHEDDAR

PEPPER

TIP

For a bit of extra flavour, add some chopped parsley, sliced spring onion (scallion) tops or whatever herbs you fancy at the point when you stir the sour cream through the potato slices.

TINY CHEESE PIES

My father-in-law's wife, Fiorella, made these pies one of the first times I went over to their house and I remember smelling them cooking as I walked through the door and thinking, 'Wow, I am gonna love today.' She got the recipe from Donna Hay and without knowing me very well she'd already anticipated I'd ask for it and had a photocopy waiting on the kitchen bench! Over the years I've changed it a little to make it simpler and now I serve these as canapés when friends come over. Vegetarians in particular love them. Makes 24

Cooking time: 20 minutes | Prep time: 5 minutes

Preheat the oven to 150°C (300°F). Spray a 24-cup mini muffin tin lightly with olive oil spray.

Place the ricotta, egg, herbs and parmesan in the food processor and process until smooth.

Spoon 1½ tablespoons of the ricotta mixture into each muffin hole. Top each with a tomato quarter, a few herb leaves and a shake of salt and pepper. Bake for 15–17 minutes, or until set and golden. (If the pies are still pale on top, switch the grill (broiler) on and place the tin under it for 3–4 minutes until nicely coloured.) Remove from the oven and leave to cool slightly in the tin before serving.

OLIVE OIL SPRAY, FOR GREASING

500 G (1 LB 2 OZ) RICOTTA

1 EGG

1 GENEROUS HANDFUL OF WHATEVER SOFT HERB LEAVES YOU HAVE LYING AROUND, PLUS EXTRA TO DECORATE

100 G (3½ OZ/1 CUP) FINELY GRATED PARMESAN

8 CHERRY TOMATOES, QUARTERED

SALT AND PEPPER

TIPS

1. If you want to make these for your friends, have the mixture ready to go in the mini muffin tin and keep it in the fridge until they come over, then pop them in the oven with a timer set so that everyone gets to enjoy them hot out of the oven.

2. If you don't have any herbs in the house, celery leaves also work very nicely here.

GET STUFFED ZUCCHINI FLOWERS

Okay, I've included this recipe to show off more than anything else. Finding zucchini flowers at the same time as actually being in the mood to deep-fry them and also having some fresh ricotta lying around seems as unlikely as fitting a camel through the eye of a needle. Still. If you happen to have all three of these factors coincide, this is the only recipe you'll ever need. Simplicity is the key to unlocking the best from these very good ingredients. Serves 6–7

Cooking time: 5 minutes | Prep time: 15 minutes

Combine all the filling ingredients together in a bowl. Stuff the flowers by carefully opening up the petals and putting a generous blob of the filling mixture inside, then closing them up and giving the petals a light twist to seal.

Make the batter by combining all the ingredients in a large bowl. The batter should be nice and light, about the consistency of a yoghurt drink – if it's looking too thick, add a splash more water.

Fill a large saucepan with oil and heat it to 180°C (350°F), or until the point where a chopstick or spoon lowered into the oil bubbles away merrily.

Dip the zucchini flowers into the batter to coat, then hold them above the bowl to allow any excess batter to drip off before lowering them into the sizzling oil. (Around this point you will probably start to realise that zucchini flowers are more robust than they appear and can take the handling and frying!) Fry for 2 minutes per side, then remove them with a slotted spoon and drain on paper towel. Serve immediately with a light salad, lemon wedges and fancy salt.

20 ZUCCHINI (COURGETTE) FLOWERS, WITH BABY ZUCCHINI ATTACHED

CANOLA OIL, FOR DEEP-FRYING

FILLING

250 G (9 OZ/1 CUP) RICOTTA

¼ BUNCH PARSLEY, FINELY CHOPPED

2 TABLESPOONS FINELY CHOPPED SPRING ONIONS (SCALLIONS), GREEN TOPS ONLY

BATTER

250 ML (8½ FL OZ/1 CUP) COLD WATER, PLUS EXTRA IF NECESSARY

125 G (4½ OZ/1 CUP) CORNFLOUR (CORNSTARCH)

150 G (5½ OZ/1 CUP) SELF-RAISING FLOUR

PINCH OF SALT

TO SERVE

SALAD LEAVES

LEMON WEDGES

SEA SALT FLAKES

SCALLOPS ON THE SHELL

A good friend who was closing her restaurant for the Christmas to New Year break once gave me all the scallops she had because she didn't want them to go to waste. There were containers and containers of them and they were the finest quality. I tried cooking them all different ways and what I discovered was that the simplest and easiest method was the best. And now scallops always remind me of Christmas. Serves 4

Cooking time: 3–6 minutes | Prep time: 5 minutes

Preheat the grill (broiler) as hot as it can go.

Put the bread in the food processor together with the butter, garlic, salt and parsley, if using. Whizz everything together to a rough crumb.

Arrange the scallop shells on a baking tray and top each with ¾ teaspoon of the crumb mixture.

Place the tray under the grill and cook for 3–5 minutes, or until the crumb is nicely golden but not dark brown (you'll want to keep an eye on them as this can turn quickly). Serve immediately with the lemon wedges.

250 G (9 OZ) SOURDOUGH BREAD (CRUSTS OK), TORN INTO PIECES

50 G (1¾ OZ) BEST-QUALITY BUTTER

1 TABLESPOON WHIPPED GARLIC OR 1 FINELY GRATED SMALL GARLIC CLOVE

¼ TEASPOON SALT

1 TABLESPOON ROUGHLY CHOPPED PARSLEY (OPTIONAL)

12 SCALLOPS ON THE SHELL

2 LEMONS, CUT INTO WEDGES

TIP

This crumb mixture is delicious and it will be tempting to add extra but trust me, having cooked this many times, it is better to leave your audience wanting more. Any left-over mix can always be popped in a zip-lock bag, labelled and frozen for later use – or try it toasted in a 200°C (400°F) oven for 5-7 minutes and sprinkled over pasta.

LOBSTER HAND ROLLS

When I was a kid, my dad was involved in rock lobster fishing down in a South Australian town called Robe. He would bring home lobsters and my mum would experiment with different ways to prepare and serve them, but no matter what she tried, no matter what was fashionable or what was going on in fancy restaurants, this was always the method she would return to and that us kids requested. It is really easy but, more importantly, it gives the limelight to the star ingredient. Serves 6–8

Cooking time: n/a | Prep time: 10 minutes

Have an enormous serving platter ready and decorate it with salad greens, flowers, leaves from the garden ... whatever excites you.

Wash the guts out of the lobster, then pull out the flesh as neatly as possible and slice it on a clean chopping board.

Return the flesh to the two half-shells of the lobster in as close to the original position as you can and lay them out on the serving platter.

Divide the nori pieces among small serving plates and the rice among small serving bowls. Fill a few small dipping bowls with soy sauce.

Place the lobster platter in the middle of the table for everyone to help themselves. To eat, pick up a piece of seaweed, top it with rice (a generous tablespoon), add a piece of the lobster dipped briefly into the soy sauce (don't drown it!) and finish with a dab of wasabi, then close the bundle and pop it into your mouth. Repeat.

1 × 2 KG (4 LB 6 OZ) FRESHLY COOKED ROCK LOBSTER (SEE COOK'S NOTE BELOW), CUT IN HALF LENGTHWAYS

6–8 BEST-QUALITY NORI SEAWEED SHEETS, EACH CUT INTO 8 PIECES

550 G (1 LB 3 OZ/3 CUPS) HOT ABSORPTION-METHOD COOKED RICE (SEE PAGE 13)

JAPANESE SOY SAUCE, TO SERVE

WASABI, TO SERVE

SALAD GREENS, FLOWERS AND LEAVES, TO DECORATE

TIPS

1. If you are lucky enough to have a fresh, live lobster to hand, then kill it humanely and boil it whole for 10 minutes for every kilo of weight. Otherwise, buy a cooked one from your fishmonger and eat it the day you buy it.

2. Don't be afraid to outsource your rice cooking if you're on holidays or just can't be bothered. All good Asian takeaway joints will sell you good, hot rice cheap.

PAN-FRIED SARDINES

People talk in hushed tones about sardines. They're a cult food. For years I was intimidated by them – so small, so fishy, so culty. I thought maybe I needed a nonna to have handed me down a recipe and that to cook them right I needed more ethnicity, more reverence and a sprinkling of holy oil. Not so. The reason they're so revered is because they're tasty, healthy, delicious and require zero fucks. Serves 4

Cooking time: 10 minutes | Prep time: 5 minutes

To make the tahini-garlic sauce, whizz all the ingredients together in a food processor until smooth. Set aside.

Heat the olive oil in a non-stick frying pan over a medium heat. Add the sardines, skin side down, and cook for 3 minutes.

While the sardines are cooking, get everything else ready. Pop the bread in the toaster, divide the salad leaves among serving plates and top with the tomatoes and buffalo mozzarella pieces.

Carefully flip the sardines and fry for another 2–3 minutes until looking opaque and a bit sexy and golden. Serve alongside the salad and the toast, topped with a generous blob of the tahini-garlic sauce.

TIP

The tahini-garlic sauce here is something that I also like to use on barbecued vegetables like eggplant (aubergine) and zucchini (courgette). This recipe makes more than you need – it keeps in an airtight container in the fridge for up to 1 week.

2 TEASPOONS OLIVE OIL

20 FRESH SARDINE FILLETS

4 PIECES SOURDOUGH BREAD

2 LARGE HANDFULS MIXED SALAD LEAVES

20 SEMI-DRIED (SUN-BLUSHED) TOMATOES

2 × 125 G (4½ OZ) BUFFALO MOZZARELLA BALLS, TORN INTO PIECES

TAHINI-GARLIC SAUCE

200 G (7 OZ) GREEK-STYLE YOGHURT

80 G (2¾ OZ/½ CUP) CASHEW NUTS

1 SMALL GARLIC CLOVE, CRUSHED

1 TEASPOON HONEY

½ TEASPOON SALT

JUICE OF 1 LEMON

50 G (1¾ OZ) TAHINI

½ BUNCH MINT LEAVES

DEEP-FRIED WHITEBAIT (A.K.A. 'FISH CHIPS')

Whenever our local fish place has whitebait I abandon whatever I had planned for dinner and schedule this in immediately because it's so easy and everyone thinks it's the best. The whitebait needs no preparation and can be eaten head, guts and all, which takes 'nose-to-tail eating' back from the hipster chefs! Kids will follow your lead here, so if they see you eating this with calm gusto, it won't even occur to them to think it's gross. Serves 6

Cooking time: 5 minutes | Prep time: 5 minutes

Dry the whitebait off on the paper it came wrapped in.

Fill a large saucepan with canola oil and heat it to deep-frying temperature, about 180°C (350°F). (You can check this by placing a wooden chopstick or the handle of a wooden spoon into the centre of the oil. If it's at deep-frying temperature, it should start a regular, pleasant boil. If it bubbles furiously, the oil is too hot.)

Combine the flour and paprika in a large metal bowl. Add the whitebait and toss to coat.

Deep-fry the whitebait for 2–3 minutes in small batches until golden and crispy, draining on paper towel and keeping the cooked fish warm in a low oven as you go.

Sprinkle with salt then serve immediately with generous wedges of lemon, Kewpie mayonnaise and rice. If anyone at your table is squeamish about eating whole fish, give them permission to drown the fishies in tomato sauce.

350 G (12½ OZ) FRESH WHITEBAIT

CANOLA OIL, FOR DEEP-FRYING

75 G (2¾ OZ/½ CUP) PLAIN (ALL-PURPOSE) FLOUR

1 TABLESPOON SWEET PAPRIKA

SALT

TO SERVE

LEMON WEDGES

KEWPIE MAYONNAISE

ABSORPTION-METHOD COOKED RICE (SEE PAGE 13)

TOMATO SAUCE (OPTIONAL)

NO-FAIL BEER-BATTERED FISH

I once had a flatmate who left without telling anyone, leaving behind his bed along with the stash of magazines hidden under it. He was a chef and cooked beer-battered fish and chips for us once, which was mind-blowing as at the time we were existing on 2-minute noodles and tins of tuna. I forget his name but I will never, ever forget how good it is to eat your own home-cooked fish 'n' chips. Serves 6

Cooking time: 10–15 minutes | Prep time: 5 minutes

Sift the flour, salt and paprika into a large bowl and add a few good grinds of pepper. Pop the top of your beer and gradually whisk it into the flour, slowly digging deep into the mixture with your whisk to thin it out until the batter flows a little but is still heavy enough to easily stick to a piece of fish. (Don't stress about the lumps – if you sifted the flour first then they should cook out.)

Preheat a grill (broiler) to low and have paper towels standing by and your plates ready to go.

Fill a large saucepan with canola oil and heat it to deep-frying temperature. (You can check this by placing a wooden chopstick or the handle of a wooden spoon into the centre of the oil. If it's at deep-frying temperature, it should start a regular, pleasant boil. If it bubbles furiously the oil is too hot.)

Dip the fish fillets into the batter, then slowly lower half the fillets into the oil one at a time, being careful not to crowd the pan. Cook each side for 3 minutes, then keep warm under a preheated grill. Cook the second batch and serve immediately with chips, lemon wedges and a handful of salad leaves.

250 G (9 OZ/1⅔ CUPS) SELF-RAISING FLOUR, SIFTED

¼ TEASPOON SALT

½ TEASPOON SWEET PAPRIKA

FRESHLY GROUND BLACK PEPPER

300 ML (10 FL OZ) COLD BEER

CANOLA OIL, FOR DEEP-FRYING

6 FLATHEAD FILLETS OR OTHER FIRM WHITE FISH FILLETS (E.G. SNAPPER OR LING)

TO SERVE

CHIPS

LEMON WEDGES

SALAD LEAVES

TIP

There is no shame in buying hot chips from the shop to accompany this meal or even better (and cheaper!), using pre-cut, oven-bake chips from the freezer section of the supermarket.

WHOLE RAINBOW TROUT

Cooking whole fish on top of a wire rack is a real revelation – it stops the fish from sticking but gives it enough air to crisp up the skin. Australian rainbow trout is famous around the world for its pristine flavour. It's also unique for being affordable, sustainable and suitable for a one-fish-per-plate meal. This recipe is based on a Jamie Oliver one and is so easy you'll actually think I'm kidding. Setting a timer is key, so have your phone ready. Serves 4

Cooking time: 12 minutes | Prep time: 10 minutes

Preheat your grill (broiler) to maximum. Arrange the shelves in the oven so that the fish, sitting on a rack over an oven tray, will sit about 15 cm (6 in) from the element.

Cut 5 mm (¼ in) slashes into both sides of each trout with a knife, about 5 each side. Rub the slashes and skin with the whipped garlic and olive oil and season with salt and pepper, then stuff the cavities with the chopped parsley. Place the fish side by side on a wire rack that sits neatly over an oven tray.

Zest the lemons over the fish and slice two of the lemons, stuffing the slices into the fish cavities. Halve the remaining lemons and place them cut side up on the tray with the fish.

Dot the trout with the butter and place it under the grill. Cook for 12 minutes, turning halfway through cooking, until crispy and golden. Serve immediately, squeezing the cooked lemon over the top once the fish are plated.

4 × 700 G (1 LB 9 OZ) WHOLE RAINBOW TROUT

2 TABLESPOONS WHIPPED GARLIC OR 2 FINELY GRATED SMALL GARLIC CLOVES

4 TABLESPOONS OLIVE OIL

SALT AND PEPPER

2 TABLESPOONS CHOPPED PARSLEY, BASIL OR CELERY LEAVES

4 LEMONS

100 G (3½ OZ) COLD BUTTER, CUT INTO SLIVERS

SUKIYAKI (A.K.A. JAPANESE HOTPOT)

I can't tell you enough how delicious this meal is! It's so tasty and shared and delightful, it creates what the Danes call 'hygge' (warm togetherness) and it makes your house smell like Japan. When I was a kid my parents used to cook this for dinner parties in the small Australian town where we grew up. Their friends would come over on wintry nights and sit on the floor around a low Japanese table and get red in the face from the heat from the cooker and all the wine. Serves 6–8

Cooking time: as long as you want to keep eating | Prep time: 15 minutes

To make the sukiyaki sauce, combine all the ingredients except the stock or water in a jug and stir.

Have all your hotpot ingredients prepared and placed in food-group clusters on a serving platter except for the meat, which should have its own platter.

In the middle of the dining table, heat up a large cast-iron casserole pot or heavy-based frying pan using a single-element camping stove.

Use the fattiest piece of meat to rub on the hot pan as it heats up, then start placing a cupful or so of each ingredient into the pan in the order of how long they will take to cook, starting with the leeks and leaving it for 2 minutes, then following with the tofu, beef, mushrooms, noodles and, finally, the cabbage. Pour over half the sukiyaki sauce, bring to a gentle simmer and cook, without stirring, for 5 minutes.

Serve a small bowl of hot rice per person and have everyone crack one raw egg each into a second bowl. The idea is that you take a few pieces of food out of the hotpot and dip them in the raw egg and the heat from the food cooks a tiny layer of egg onto the food. Then you place the food on the rice and eat it with the rice.

Relax, allow the food time to cook and slowly, over the course of the meal, keep topping up the hotpot with the raw ingredients. Midway through the meal you may wish to offer a top-up of rice to guests or even a second egg. You will also need to top up the hotpot with the rest of the sukiyaki sauce as it starts to look dry, adding the stock or water to the sauce a few splashes at a time if it has become too concentrated.

If there is still leftover raw food and everyone is full, add it all into the pot, give it 3 minutes, then switch off the heat and ignore it until everyone has gone home. The cooked food inside the hotpot makes great bento box fillers.

400–500 G (14 OZ–1 LB 2 OZ) FILLET STEAK, FINELY SLICED

1 LEEK, WASHED, TRIMMED AND CUT INTO 7 CM (2¾ IN) BATONS

500 G (1 LB 2 OZ) MEDIUM FIRMNESS TOFU, CUT INTO 2 CM (¾ IN) CUBES

600 G (1 LB 5 OZ) MIXED MUSHROOMS (OYSTER, ENOKI, AND SHIITAKE)

400 G (14 OZ) YAM OR POTATO NOODLES

¼ CHINESE CABBAGE (WOMBOK), CUT INTO 2 CM (¾ IN) PIECES

SUKIYAKI SAUCE

250 ML (8½ FL OZ/1 CUP) JAPANESE SOY SAUCE

250 ML (8½ FL OZ/1 CUP) SAKÈ

250 ML (8½ FL OZ/1 CUP) MIRIN

60 G (2 OZ) CASTER (SUPERFINE) SUGAR

500 ML (17 FL OZ/2 CUPS) VEGETABLE STOCK OR WATER

TO SERVE

ABSORPTION-METHOD COOKED RICE (SEE PAGE 13)

1 RAW EGG PER PERSON

TIPS

1. Camping stoves can be bought inexpensively from outdoor adventure shops or hardware stores. In the past I have also successfully used a kerosene stove and, on other occasions, an electric frying pan with an extension cord to the table. If you don't have any of these things, it works to cook this meal on a large frying pan on the stove top although your family/guests will not be able to watch the food cooking.

2. If you're feeding a lot of meat lovers, you might want to add another 350 g (12½ oz) of steak. And speaking of steak, the way to get the thinnest slice of meat is to freeze the steak for 3 hours before slicing.

3. I love to use shiitake and enoki mushrooms in this dish but it is fine to use button mushrooms or whatever your local grocer has in stock.

THE SACRIFICIAL CARROT PORK BELLY

I've cooked a lot of pork belly in my time and there's a recurring problem: the lengthy cooking time creates the most lovely, moist and tender belly meat, the top is protected by the skin (which should go crunchy and delicious if done right) but the bottom tends to burn. Thankfully, I've arrived at a solution – the sacrificial carrot. By effectively using a sliced carrot as a trivet, the carrot burns but the bottom of the pork piece does not. Are you comfortable with wasting a carrot? I am.

It might be worth keeping this recipe a secret, so your friends, family and lovers have to keep requesting it over and over again. You have to give a few fucks to get the recipe timing right the first few times (though the recipe bit itself is easy). My recommendation is – if you want this for your evening meal, start working on it around midday. Serves 6–8

Cooking time: 5 hours | Prep time: 15 minutes

Preheat the oven to 140°C (275°F) and line two roasting tins with baking paper.

Arrange the sliced carrot on one of the prepared roasting tins in a pile roughly the same size as the pork belly piece, then top with the apple, then the onion and garlic.

Using your sharpest knife, a Stanley knife or a razor blade, cut a criss-cross pattern into the pork skin. Rub a little salt into the cracks in the skin and underside of the pork and massage with a little olive oil. (If you found previous forays into the world of pork belly made you feel queasy from its richness, it might be because too much salt was added at this point. It's a common mistake. The meat itself is extremely flavoursome and doesn't need too much added.)

Place the pork on top of the vegetables then roast on a high shelf in the oven for 4½ hours, or until nicely tender. Discard the burnt carrot but set aside the onion and apple mixture and keep warm. Transfer the meat to the other prepared roasting tin and leave to rest for 20 minutes.

While the meat rests, switch the oven on to grill (broiler) and raise the temperature to 220°C (430°F).

Once rested, place the pork belly under the hot grill and cook for 5–7 minutes, or until the skin has puffed up all over like popcorn. (Be sure to keep an eye on it as you go as it can easily burn once it's puffed.) Remove from the oven and leave to rest for another 20 minutes, then slice up and serve with the veggies.

1–2 LARGE CARROTS, SLICED

1 GREEN APPLE, PEELED AND FINELY SLICED

1 LARGE ONION, FINELY SLICED

3 GARLIC CLOVES, FINELY SLICED

1 × 800 G–1.1 KG (1 LB 12 OZ–2 LB 7 OZ) PIECE PORK BELLY, AT ROOM TEMPERATURE

¼ TEASPOON SALT

1 TABLESPOON OLIVE OIL

TIP

Leftover pork crackling will stay crisp and crunchy for longer if wrapped in a brown paper bag before refrigeration. To refresh, warm it gently under the grill.

STICKY, SEXY LAMB RIBS

I've tried cooking lamb ribs a bunch of ways – if you look up recipes on the internet a lot of them would have you slow cooking them in stock for hours. I've done this but found the liquid robs the meat of its natural flavour. A slow, dry roast keeps all the goodness within, and a hot finish helps caramelise the outer layer, giving you a chewy, juicy finish. Just allow yourself plenty of time. Serves 4

Cooking time: 2 hours 40 minutes | Prep time: 5 minutes

Preheat the oven to 140°C (275°F). Line two baking trays with baking paper.

In a large bowl, combine the spices, salt and garlic. Add the lamb ribs and coat them in the mixture, then spread the ribs out on the prepared baking trays and roast for 2½ hours, or until tender.

Heat the grill (broiler) to 220°C (430°F) and line another baking tray with baking paper. If the ribs are not already cut into single fingers, do this now.

Brush the ribs generously with barbecue sauce (I use regular supermarket barbecue sauce but there are all kinds of fancy ones out there you might want to try) and grill on a high shelf in the oven for 10 minutes until bubbling and lightly charred. Sprinkle over the lemon zest and serve with fat lemon wedges.

2 TABLESPOONS PAPRIKA

2 TABLESPOONS GROUND CUMIN

2 TABLESPOONS SUMAC

1 TEASPOON SALT

2 TABLESPOONS WHIPPED GARLIC OR 2 FINELY GRATED SMALL GARLIC CLOVES

2 KG (4 LB 6 OZ) LAMB RIBLETS

250 ML (8½ FL OZ/1 CUP) YOUR FAVOURITE BARBECUE SAUCE

ZEST OF 1 LEMON, PLUS EXTRA LEMON WEDGES TO SERVE

TIPS

1. The slow roasting of the ribs can be done up to 2 days before the final grilling – make them up in advance and store them in an airtight container in the fridge until needed.

2. Any leftover ribs are great cold as part of a ploughman's lunch or portioned up in tupperware with rice.

ZERO F*CKS
SWEET STUFF

Desserts weren't common in my childhood home. Sometimes we'd get ice cream, once in a while we'd get jelly or, very occasionally, a pudding, which was hot and so special that we'd all lose our minds and burn the roofs of our mouths. Nowadays with four children to feed I make a dessert every second night, because a kid who might not be digging the main meal will at least get some nutrients from the sweet stuff. And when people come over? I got that shit covered.

SISTERHOOD SCONES

Scones have a mythical quality to them. It always seemed to me that only old-fashioned people could make scones, and they were (almost always) women. Women who were so old they could remember milk coming in glass bottles, travelling by horse, or dating before Tinder, booty calls and eyelash perms.

I think scones are magical, and therefore they need to have a special magical ingredient. That special magical ingredient is lemonade, and what makes it so wonderful is that the cheaper the lemonade, the better. Little warning: a scone can't really ever pretend to be good for you. It's not. But it is good for your soul, and great for long afternoons with mugs of hot tea and friends. Makes about 16 scones

Cooking time: 12–15 minutes | Prep time: 5 minutes

Preheat the oven to 250°C (480°F). Line a baking tray with baking paper.

Add all the ingredients to a mixing bowl and quickly combine, pretending that mixing motions are under strict rations and you can't use too many. (The key to making scones successfully is to do everything as though you're in a mad hurry.) When you think it's probably not mixed enough and needs a dozen more stirs, stop.

Tip the mixture out onto a well-floured bench and pat it into a circle about 2 cm (¾ in) thick.

Quickly cut the mixture out into circles with a scone ring, or into lovely triangles of dough if using a knife (don't worry if they're uneven, it doesn't matter). Avoid kneading any left-over bits and – with as little handling as possible – fashion them into whatever shape you think is acceptable.

Transfer your scones to the prepared tray. Trusted women explain that arranging them so that they lightly touch helps them gather one another up to rise together. Bake for 12–15 minutes, or until the scones are golden on top and feel light and hollow if you tap them.

While the scones are baking, whip your cream, being careful to stop while it still looks a little shiny and gloopy. (You don't want it stiff like butter, you want it custardy and sexy.) And get the kettle on for a big pot of strong tea.

Remove the scones from the oven and eat warm with friends, serving with generous helpings of cream and jam, lots of hot tea and something funky on the stereo.

750 G (1 LB 11 OZ/5 CUPS) SELF-RAISING FLOUR, SIFTED

250 G (9 OZ/1 CUP) SOUR CREAM

400 ML (13½ FL OZ) CHEAP LEMONADE, AT ROOM TEMPERATURE

PINCH OF SALT

TO SERVE

WHIPPING CREAM

TEA

BEST-QUALITY HOME-MADE JAM

MILKY CARAMEL PECAN SLICE

This is a way to eat condensed milk without feeling guilty. The slice has nuts in it and therefore counts as both a protein and a health food! It's also a cinch to put together. Makes 24 slices

Cooking time: 25 minutes | Prep time: 5 minutes

Line a 23 cm (9 in) square brownie tin with baking paper.

Put all the base ingredients except the flour into a food processor and whizz until the mix resembles breadcrumbs. Add the flour, then whizz for just a few seconds until everything comes together in a sticky ball.

Roughly press the base mixture into the tin, then transfer to the fridge to firm.

Preheat the oven to 175°C (345°F).

Add all the topping ingredients except the pecans to a very clean non-stick frying pan and bring to a gentle simmer. Cook, stirring continuously, for 10 minutes until reduced by about a third. (It doesn't really change colour, so setting a timer here is important.)

Remove the tin from the fridge and flatten the base dough evenly across the bottom (don't worry about it being perfect – no one sees it). Working quickly, stir the pecans through the caramel topping mixture then pour the whole lot over the base, levelling it off with the back of a spoon.

Bake in the oven for 15 minutes, or until the top has bubbled and browned just slightly. Leave to cool, then transfer to the fridge for 2 hours to firm before cutting into fingers using a sharp knife.

TIPS

1. Try replacing 50 g (1¾ oz) of pecans with 50 g (1¾ oz) of macadamia nuts. Very delicious!

2. If you can't wait for the slice to chill in the fridge after baking you can attack it straight away – it just won't cut neatly.

BASE

½ TEASPOON CREAM OF TARTAR

½ TEASPOON BICARBONATE OF SODA (BAKING SODA)

50 G (1¾ OZ/½ CUP) CASHEW NUTS

¼ TEASPOON SALT

50 ML (1¾ FL OZ) MAPLE SYRUP OR RICE MALT SYRUP

90 G (3 OZ) BUTTER

1 EGG

150 G (5½ OZ/1 CUP) PLAIN (ALL-PURPOSE) FLOUR

MILKY CARAMEL TOPPING

1 × 325 G (11½ OZ) TIN SWEETENED CONDENSED MILK

60 G (2 OZ) BUTTER

75 G (2¾ OZ) SOFT BROWN SUGAR

1 TEASPOON VANILLA PASTE

2 TABLESPOONS MAPLE OR RICE MALT SYRUP

300 G (10½ OZ/3 CUPS) PECANS

SUPERMUM COOKIES

When I was a kid my neighbour Kate had a cookie jar that was always full of something homemade. I thought her mum, Marg, was a goddess. Now I can be like her because I make batches of this cookie dough and keep it in the freezer, then slice off discs of it whenever I have people around for tea or meetings. They taste good and they're always fresh. Makes about 70 cookies

Cooking time: 10–12 minutes | Prep time: 15 minutes, plus chilling and freezing

Cream the butter and sugar together in an electric mixer until thoroughly combined, then beat in the zest followed by the eggs, one at a time. Sift in the flours and mix until combined then use you hands to stir through the nuts and choc chips evenly. Divide the dough into four evenly sized portions.

Shape one of the dough portions into a 30 cm (12 in) log and place it on a sheet of baking paper. Roll it up neat, tight and cylindrical (like a dead body in a carpet), then twist the ends of the baking paper together at each end to seal. Repeat with the remaining cookie dough. Put three of the logs in the freezer for later and the fourth in the fridge to chill and firm – after 3 hours the fridge cookie log should be ready to slice.

Preheat the oven to 180°C (350°F) and line a baking tray with baking paper.

Slice the cookie log into slices no thicker than than 4 mm (¼ in) and lay them out on the prepared baking tray, leaving a little space between each to allow room for them to expand. Bake for 10–12 minutes or until golden around the edges. Eat within 4 days.

500 G (1 LB 2 OZ) BUTTER, AT ROOM TEMPERATURE

325 G (11½ OZ/1⅓ CUPS) CASTER (SUPERFINE) SUGAR

ZEST OF 1 LEMON, ORANGE OR TANGELO

2 EGGS, BEATEN

250 G (9 OZ/1⅔ CUPS) PLAIN (ALL-PURPOSE) FLOUR

300 G (10½ OZ/2 CUPS) SELF-RAISING FLOUR

200 G (7 OZ/2 CUPS) WALNUTS, ROUGHLY CHOPPED

60 G (2 OZ/⅓ CUP) CHOCOLATE CHIPS

TIPS

1. Try swapping out the walnuts for pecans, peanut butter or dried figs.

2. Sometimes I roll the log in polenta, sesame seeds or desiccated coconut. Experiment – this recipe is extremely forgiving.

3. Cutting the dough logs from frozen will shatter the discs but don't stress – they will still form cookie-shapes during the baking process.

THE ONLY BANANA BREAD RECIPE YOU'LL EVER NEED

Are you like me and go scrambling for a banana bread recipe every time your fruit bowl starts to turn brown? For years I had no memory for a recipe and had to search for one afresh each time. So annoying! Save yourself the scramble and keep this one handy. It's ridiculously easy. Makes 1 loaf

Cooking time: 50 minutes | Prep time: 10 minutes

Preheat the oven to 175°C (345°F). Line a regular loaf (bar) tin with baking paper and give the paper a light spray with oil.

Combine all the ingredients except the flour and nuts in a food processor and whizz until combined. Add the flour and blitz for 7 seconds, then lightly stir through the nuts, if using. Scrape the mix into the loaf tin.

Bake in the oven for 50 minutes, or until a skewer inserted into the centre of the loaf comes out clean. Remove from the oven and leave to cool slightly in the tin for 5 minutes before turning out. Eat warm with lots of butter.

TIPS

1. The flavour of this banana bread improves over time! Toast or grill (broil) it to freshen it up.

2. This freezes really well when wrapped thoroughly in plastic wrap, however defrosting it takes a day in the fridge. If you're not sure of when your emergency might arise and you might need it quickly, slice the loaf before freezing, keeping the pieces wrapped separately. You can then toast the individual slices from frozen.

OLIVE OIL SPRAY, FOR GREASING

3 DISGUSTINGLY RIPE BANANAS (ABOUT 250 G/9 OZ)

60 G (2 OZ) BUTTER, SOFTENED

90 ML (3 FL OZ) LIQUID COCONUT OIL OR FRESH-TASTING OLIVE OIL

250 G (9 OZ) SUGAR (ANY KIND = OK)

¼ TEASPOON GROUND NUTMEG (OPTIONAL)

1 TEASPOON GROUND CINNAMON (OPTIONAL)

2 EGGS

1 TEASPOON BAKING POWDER

1 TEASPOON BICARBONATE OF SODA (BAKING SODA)

100 ML (3½ FL OZ) MILK

1 TEASPOON WHITE VINEGAR

PINCH OF SALT

250 G (9 OZ/1⅔ CUPS) PLAIN (ALL-PURPOSE) FLOUR

100 G (3½ OZ/1 CUP) WALNUTS OR PECANS, LIGHTLY CHOPPED (OPTIONAL)

LEGIT MUG CAKE

Making a cake in a mug is kind of a modern fad and is a great idea – on paper. My main problem with it is that a good cake usually requires egg and all the mug cake recipes I've ever read use a whole one for one tiny little cake. That's way too eggy for my liking. So I've taken the mixing and the stirring out of the mug and into a bigger bowl, leaving you with more servings than you can probably use, which is fine because the storing and the saving and the using later is almost as cool as the cake itself. Makes 6–8 mug cakes

Cooking time: 1–2 minutes | Prep time: 5 minutes

Chuck all the ingredients except the flour and berries into the food processor and whizz everything together to combine, then remove the blade, add the flour and mix through with a metal spoon to form a stiff batter.

Spoon 100 g (3½ oz) of the batter mixture into a mug, then press 5 blueberries down into the batter. Repeat with as many mugs as you want to make, setting aside the leftover mixture for later use (see Tip 1).

Transfer the mug cakes to the microwave and cook one at a time for 1½ minutes on high – you can tell when they're cooked because they look firm on top and smell awesome. (If you overcook them, they go nasty and rock-like.)

Serve hot with cream, vanilla ice cream or both.

TIPS

1. For the leftover mixture, spray a muffin tin with cooking oil. Spoon 100 g (3½ oz) of the batter into as many muffin holes as you have leftover mix and freeze until required. Once frozen, loosen and pop the batter discs out with a butter knife and store in a zip-lock bag in the freezer until required. Nuking the cakes from frozen works (it's some sort of microwave magic) and does not require extra time.

2. If you want fruit in your mug cake, dice up the frozen cake and toss it around with berries or cooked apple (you can also add these before freezing if you want).

100 G (3½ OZ) BUTTER, AT ROOM TEMPERATURE

100 G (3½ OZ) CASTER SUGAR

1 EGG

1 TABLESPOON VANILLA PASTE

2 TABLESPOONS SOUR CREAM

100 G (3½ OZ/1 CUP) GROUND ALMONDS

60 ML (2 FL OZ/¼ CUP) MILK

¼ TEASPOON SALT

½ TEASPOON BAKING POWDER

100 G (3½ OZ/⅔ CUP) SELF-RAISING FLOUR

150 G (5½ OZ) BLUEBERRIES

CREAM AND/OR VANILLA ICE CREAM, TO SERVE

EMERGENCY CRUMBLE

I always keep a zip-lock bag of this crumble topping in the freezer and a tin of fruit in the cupboard so hot dessert at my place is never more than 15 minutes away. Crumble is one of the few desserts where you are meant to crunch on undissolved sugar granules as you eat. For this reason, I encourage you to experiment with different sugars. It's rather delicious. Makes 1 crumble (and enough topping for 2 emergencies)

Cooking time: 15 minutes | Prep time: 10 minutes

Whisk the egg yolk, vanilla, sour cream and water together in a small jug with a fork.

Add all the other ingredients except the tinned fruit to a food processor and blitz together for 30 seconds, pouring over the egg mixture as you go, until the colour of the mix looks uniform (being careful not to overmix). This is your crumble mix.

Preheat the grill (broiler) to medium. Grease an ovenproof gratin dish with a little butter.

Drain your tinned fruit and plop it into the prepared dish. Sprinkle with a little extra ground cinnamon if desired, then top with as much crumble mix as looks right – a quarter to a third of the mixture, in my experience. Store the left-over crumble mix in a labelled zip-lock bag in the freezer for next time (and remember that a bag of this good stuff plus a tin of fruit is a perfectly acceptable gift for a new mother).

Place under the grill and cook for 15 minutes or until golden brown, checking regularly to ensure it doesn't burn. Serve with vanilla ice cream and/or fresh cream.

TIPS

1. The uncooked, crumbly mixture doubles as a cookie dough that can be sprinkled raw onto ice cream or just eaten out of the bag. (Sorry.)

2. Purists argue that good crumbles require oats and, though one of the original reasons I wanted to write this recipe was to leave them out to create a cakey, short-bread-like crumble, once in a while I crave their humble, chewy presence. If you feel the same, just substitute 50 g (1¾ oz) of rolled (porridge) oats for the same quantity of flour, mixing it through before the wet mixture goes in.

2 EGG YOLKS

1 TEASPOON VANILLA PASTE

2 TABLESPOONS SOUR CREAM OR THICKENED (WHIPPING) CREAM

2 TABLESPOONS ICY COLD WATER

200 G (7 OZ) CHILLED BUTTER, CUT INTO SLICES

400 G (14 OZ/2⅔ CUPS) PLAIN (ALL-PURPOSE) FLOUR

¼ TEASPOON SALT

1 TEASPOON GROUND CINNAMON, PLUS EXTRA FOR SPRINKLING

100 G (3½ OZ) SOFT BROWN SUGAR OR OTHER SUGAR (E.G. COCONUT SUGAR, DEMERARA SUGAR, ETC.)

100 G (3½ OZ) WHITE SUGAR

825 G (1 LB 13 OZ) TINNED FRUIT (E.G. PEAR, APPLE OR PEACHES)

TO SERVE

VANILLA ICE CREAM AND/OR FRESH CREAM

CHEAT'S TIRAMISU

I love the taste of simple, delicious ingredients. Freshly whipped cream is one of my favourites – it's always so luxurious and yummy but is also so simple. And it's also impossible to muck up.

In traditional tiramisu the creamy white part is made using whipped egg whites mixed with mascarpone cheese. My cheat's version simplifies the whole process way down; there is no egg and no expensive fresh cheese and, quite frankly, I don't care. I still think it's marvellous. But one thing you can't cheat is the overnight soaking process – this must be made the day before serving. Serves 8

Cooking time: none | Prep time: 20 minutes, plus overnight soaking

Add the cream and sugar to an electric mixer and beat until airy and light but not too stiff – you want a bit of slop left in it.

Have a clean, rectangular container ready. (I use a gorgeous square glass vase when I make this for my mum's mah-jong parties, which looks very fancy, but my Italian friend Maria uses an old baking tray – it really doesn't matter what you use.) Boil the kettle.

Add the coffee powder to a bowl and cover with 500 ml (17 fl oz/ 2 cups) of boiling water. Stir in the liqueur, if using, then dip the non-sugary side of a biscuit very briefly into the coffee – you want it to suck up some of the coffee but not get to the point where it turns to mush in your fingers – then place it, coffee side down, in your container. Repeat until you have a layer of coffee-soaked biscuits covering the base.

Top the bikkies with a generous layer of the whipped cream, then repeat the layers with a second layer of coffee-dipped biscuits and another layer of the cream. Depending on your container size, you may have enough room for a third layer of each, just be sure you have enough cream to make up a final layer.

Tidy up the sides of your container to remove any splodges of cream, then grate the dark chocolate over the top (I like to use a microplane grater for this). Cover the lot in plastic wrap and serve the following day alongside fresh strawberries.

600 ML (20½ FL OZ) THICKENED (WHIPPING) CREAM

80 G (2¾ OZ/⅓ CUP) CASTER (SUPERFINE) SUGAR OR RICE MALT SYRUP

4 TEASPOONS INSTANT COFFEE POWDER

A SPLASH OF BOOZE LIKE KAHLUA, BAILEY'S OR TIA MARIA (OPTIONAL)

250 G (9 OZ) SAVOIARDI (LADYFINGER) BISCUITS (THEY SOUND FANCY BUT ARE AVAILABLE IN EVERY MAINSTREAM SUPERMARKET)

65 G (2¼ OZ) FINEST-QUALITY DARK CHOCOLATE

STRAWBERRIES, TO SERVE

TIPS

1. Traditional tiramisu recipes top the cake with bitter cocoa – I prefer the luxurious melt of grated chocolate on my tongue, but try it with cocoa if that works better for you.

2. Any left-over biscuits and cream can be used to make little mini tubs of tiramisu for school or office lunches.

RICOTTA AND RASPBERRY PUDDING

After I nailed this recipe I googled 'ricotta pudding' and the only results listed were chocolate puddings. That made me so happy! This is my dream dessert, it reads like a wishlist of all my favourite things and what's more, it's super easy to make. Serves 8

Cooking time: 30 minutes | Prep time: 15 minutes

Preheat the oven to 160°C (320°F). Spray a 26 cm × 34 cm (10¼ in × 13½ in) ovenproof dish with oil spray or rub with butter.

Whisk the egg yolks together with the sugar and lemon zest in a large mixing bowl until pale. Whisk in the ricotta, milk, lemon juice, and melted butter to combine, then sift over the self-raising flour and mix for 2 minutes until almost smooth but still with a few lumps.

In a clean mixing bowl of a stand mixer, beat the egg whites together with 2 tablespoons of sugar until stiff, shiny peaks form. Fold half of the egg white mixture through the yolk and flour mixture, then add the remainder, folding gently so as not to bash the air out.

Boil the kettle.

Scrape the pudding batter into the prepared dish and dot all over with the raspberries, poking them in a bit if they refuse to sink. Set the dish into a larger roasting tin, pop both in the oven and fill the tray with boiling water from the kettle.

Bake for 30 minutes until puffed up, golden and still just a little wobbly in the centre. If the pudding still looks too pale on top, turn on the grill (broiler) to medium–high and give it an extra 3–4 minutes to colour (it can burn, so stay close!). Serve with vanilla ice cream.

OLIVE OIL SPRAY, FOR GREASING

4 EGGS, SEPARATED

200 G (7 OZ) CASTER (SUPERFINE) SUGAR, PLUS 2 TABLESPOONS

ZEST OF 2 LEMONS

400 G (14 OZ) FRESH RICOTTA

375 ML (12½ FL OZ/1½ CUPS) MILK

80 ML (2½ FL OZ/⅓ CUP) LEMON JUICE

150 G (5½ OZ) BUTTER, MELTED AND COOLED

150 G (5½ OZ/1 CUP) SELF-RAISING FLOUR

125 G (4½ OZ/1 CUP) RASPBERRIES

VANILLA ICE CREAM, TO SERVE

TIPS

1. This pudding is very wet the minute you take it out of the oven, but firms up over time. I like it both ways.

2. Try substituting the raspberries for blueberries or rum-soaked raisins.

CINNAMON 'TOFFEE' APPLES

This is not a toffee apple like you get on a stick. It's just permission to cook delicious cinnamony apples in a syrup that's so thick it's like toffee. And that's it – who needs anything fancier than this?

You don't need to neatly halve, quarter then evenly slice each apple here – this is tedious, time-consuming and doesn't add anything to the final product. Once your apple is peeled, just hack away at it until there's nothing left but the core. Serves 4–6

Cooking time: 15–20 minutes | Prep time: 2 minutes

Warm a very clean non-stick frying pan over a medium-high heat. Add the apple chunks to the pan with the butter and cinnamon and cook for 5 minutes until the butter has completely melted and is foaming and the apple is starting to soften.

Add the sugar and cook for another 8–12 minutes, stirring continuously, until the sugar has turned into a very thick, sticky brown toffee and the kitchen is smelling crazy good. Spoon into bowls and serve immediately with ice cream.

600 G (1 LB 5 OZ) APPLES, PEELED, ROUGHLY CHOPPED AND CORE DISCARDED

3 TABLESPOONS BUTTER

2 TEASPOONS GROUND CINNAMON

100 G (3½ OZ) BROWN OR RAPADURA SUGAR

VANILLA ICE CREAM, TO SERVE

TIP

If you want to get fancy, spoon this out into individual glasses with crushed store-bought meringue, fresh cream and a cherry on top.

NUTTY SELF-SAUCING CHOCOLATE PUDDING

My sister and I used to be nuts about self-saucing puddings. I've been making them since we were kids but my basic go-to recipe bugged me for two reasons: 1. I couldn't stop eating it even when I knew I should stop, and 2. I always thought it would be better/healthier with nuts.

After extensive experimentation in the Zero Fucks test kitchen I can confidently announce that this is the shit. It tastes kind of like if Ferrero Rochers were a hot dessert. The nuts inside make you feel full after one serve (although you still might need two) and it just feels healthier with the added protein. Don't make this if you don't like mushy, sloppy, blobby foods – this is 'pudding' in the true sense of the word. Serves 6–8

Cooking time: 30 minutes | Prep time: 10 minutes

Preheat the oven to 175°C (345°F).

Use a bowl or glass jug to melt the butter in the microwave for 30 seconds on medium. As soon as it dings, stir through the chopped chocolate so it has a chance to melt (no biggie if it doesn't all melt).

Put the brown sugar, vanilla, hazelnuts, egg, sour cream, coffee solution and melted butter-chocolate mixture in the food processor and whizz together until smooth. Add the flour and pulse until just combined, then scrape the batter into a 2 litre (68 fl oz/8 cup) ovenproof dish and smooth the top a bit to even out.

Sprinkle the cocoa and an extra 3 tablespoons of sugar over the top of the pudding, pour over the boiling water, then pop straight into the oven and bake for 30 minutes. When it's cooked the top will have risen and should feel solid and the wet sauce will be bubbling around the edges. Serve immediately with cream and ice cream.

TIPS

1. Once you've made up the batter and scraped it into the dish you can stop and refrigerate your mixture until you're ready to use for up to 3 days – this works especially well if you're bringing dessert to a family party or dropping a dessert over to a new mum. Just put the cocoa and sugar in a zip-lock bag and take it with you.

2. Try this recipe with other nuts – macadamias and almonds both work well, while a tablespoon of peanut butter in the mixture lends it a whole extra layer of nuttiness.

3. This is also still delicious the next day if you microwave each portion for 45–60 seconds and serve with ice cream.

100 G (3½ OZ) BUTTER

75 G (2¾ OZ) DARK CHOCOLATE, CHOPPED AS FINELY AS YOU CAN BE BOTHERED

100 G (3½ OZ) SOFT BROWN SUGAR, PLUS 3 TABLESPOONS FOR SPRINKLING

1 TEASPOON VANILLA PASTE

75 G (2¾ OZ) SKINNED ROASTED HAZELNUTS

1 EGG

60 G (2 OZ/¼ CUP) SOUR CREAM, CREAM OR YOGHURT

1 TEASPOON INSTANT COFFEE POWDER, DISSOLVED INTO 1 TEASPOON BOILING WATER

150 G (5½ OZ) SELF-RAISING FLOUR

1 TABLESPOON DUTCH (UNSWEETENED) COCOA POWDER

750 ML (25½ FL OZ/3 CUPS) BOILING WATER, PLUS EXTRA IF NECESSARY

TO SERVE

FRESH CREAM AND/OR VANILLA ICE CREAM

RAINY DAY TEA CAKE

Once I was so stuck for wet weather activities with my kids that we went and got the nine-year-old's ears pierced just for something to do. Now that was a good option, but she only has two ears. If you've run out of ears and are stuck indoors, this cake is a real cutie for the kids to learn on. Serves 10

Cooking time: 1 hour | Prep time: 20 minutes

Preheat the oven to 175°C (345°F). Line a 23 cm (9 in) round cake tin with baking paper.

Beat the butter and sugar together in a mixing bowl until creamy. Add one of the eggs and beat well before beating in the second.

Sift half the flour into the bowl and mix through, then stir in the milk. Add the vanilla and the remaining flour and mix together well.

Pour the batter into the prepared cake tin and bake for 1 hour or until a skewer inserted into the centre comes out clean. Remove from the oven and leave to cool slightly in the tin.

Mix all the topping ingredients together and spoon over the top of the cake, then remove the cake from the tin and leave to cool completely on a wire rack.

180 G (6½ OZ) BUTTER, AT ROOM TEMPERATURE

175 G (6 OZ/¾ CUP) CASTER (SUPERFINE) SUGAR

2 EGGS

220 G (8 OZ/1½ CUPS) SELF-RAISING FLOUR

125 ML (4 FL OZ/½ CUP) MILK

1 TEASPOON VANILLA PASTE OR ESSENCE

TOPPING

3 TABLESPOONS BUTTER, MELTED

2 TEASPOONS GROUND CINNAMON

2 TABLESPOONS CASTER (SUPERFINE) SUGAR

TIP

Kids LOVE cooking with food colouring. Make this into a version of red velvet cake by adding a tablespoon of red food colouring to the cake mix along with the milk and topping it with a half-portion of the icing from the World's Greatest Carrot Cake (page 181).

IDIOT-PROOF CHOCOLATE RIPPLE BIRTHDAY CAKE

This is the cake my kids ask for on their birthdays. They've tried many other delicious, amazing, artistic cakes but this one is their favourite! It's so easy my eyes water with gratitude. Don't muck with the proportions here (seriously, I've made this hundreds of times and it's perfect) but make it a day ahead as it needs to sit in the fridge overnight. Serves 8

Cooking time: none | Prep time: 20 minutes, plus overnight chilling

Whizz the cream and sugar together in the bowl of a mixer until thick and starting to form stiff peaks.

On the plate you intend to serve the cake on, paint two thick stripes of cream approximately double the width of your biscuits along the base.

Generously coat a biscuit with the cream and stand it up on the plate on one of the two stripes. Repeat, sandwiching the creamy biscuits together, until the stripes are covered and most of the biscuits are used (I usually have about 8 leftover).

Cover the whole lot in whatever cream remains, then carefully pop in a couple of toothpicks to keep the plastic wrap from touching the cream and refrigerate, covered, overnight.

When ready to eat, press the strawberry halves into the top and sides of the cake to cover completely, leaving a little space between each. Serve.

900 ML (30½ FL OZ) THICKENED (WHIPPING) CREAM

3 TABLESPOONS CASTER (SUPERFINE) SUGAR

250 G (9 OZ) CHOCOLATE RIPPLE BISCUITS OR OTHER PLAIN CHOCOLATE COOKIES

500 G (1 LB 2 OZ) STRAWBERRIES, HULLED AND HALVED

TIP

Whenever I make this I also make a couple of small school-lunch Tupperware serves (usually two biscuits per serve, following the method above). The kids love it.

3-HOLES VEGAN CHOCOLATE CAKE

It's always handy to have a few trusted vegan recipes up your sleeve, even if you're not even vegetarian – cooking for loved ones is about making people feel welcome, and being considerate of everyone's needs. So if someone needs their food to be vegan, that's perfectly okay with me, so long as I know some good recipe tricks. (This, by the way, is so easy and so yummy that it's my go-to chocolate cake anyway, with or without vegan friends coming over.) Why '3-holes', you ask? Please read on ... Serves 8

Cooking time: 20 minutes | Prep time: 15 minutes

Preheat the oven to 150°C (300°F). Line a 22 cm (8¾ in) round cake tin with baking paper.

In a large bowl, mix all the dry ingredients together well to combine.

Make 3 holes in the mixture: 1 large, 1 medium and 1 small hole. Into the large hole, add the melted margarine. Into the medium hole, add the vinegar. Into the small hole, add the vanilla. Pour the soy milk all over the top, then mix the whole lot together until there are no lumps.

Pour the batter out into the cake tin and bake for 18–20 minutes, or until a skewer inserted into the centre comes out clean. Remove from the oven and leave to cool completely in the tin. (Trying to take it out earlier will result in the cake breaking!)

Make the icing by mixing everything together in an electric mixer until smooth. Spread over the top of the cooled cake and decorate with berries, if desired.

TIPS

1. The brand of dairy-free margarine you use here will have a strong influence on the flavour of the icing. I use Nuttelex 'Buttery' and it's brilliant.

2. Glucose syrup is not essential for the icing but it does really help give it a glossy finish that can sometimes prove elusive when using vegan margarines.

200 G (7 OZ/1⅓ CUPS) SELF-RAISING FLOUR

100 G (3½ OZ/½ CUP) SOFT BROWN SUGAR

100 G (3½ OZ) SUGAR

50 G (1¾ OZ) DUTCH (UNSWEETENED) COCOA POWDER, SIFTED

1 TEASPOON BAKING SODA

½ TEASPOON SALT

120 G (4½ OZ) DAIRY-FREE MARGARINE, MELTED

2 TABLESPOONS WHITE OR APPLE CIDER VINEGAR

1 TEASPOON VANILLA EXTRACT

150 ML (5 FL OZ) SOY MILK OR OTHER NON-DAIRY MILK SUBSTITUTE

STRAWBERRIES, RASPBERRIES OR BLUEBERRIES, TO SERVE (OPTIONAL)

ICING

300 G (10½ OZ) ICING (CONFECTIONER'S) SUGAR

150 G (5½ OZ) DAIRY-FREE MARGARINE

2 TABLESPOONS GLUCOSE SYRUP (OPTIONAL)

1 TEASPOON BOILING WATER

WORLD'S GREATEST CARROT CAKE WITH 3-CHEESE ICING

This is it! The GREATEST! Look no further! Whooooo! What makes this cake great is the icing, which is moreish and lush, and the inherent lovely healthfulness of the cake itself, which stays moist, isn't too sweet and leaves one feeling rather jolly. If I really love you, I will make one of these for your birthday. Serves 12–15

Cooking time: 50 minutes | Prep time: 10 minutes

Preheat the oven to 160°C (320°F). Line a 24 cm (9½ in) round springform cake tin with baking paper.

Whizz the carrots and pecans together in a food processor well until they almost form a paste. Tip the mixture out into a large bowl.

Add all the other cake ingredients apart from the flour to the food processor (there's no need to wash it in between) and whiz them together, then scrape the mix into the bowl with the carrot and pecan mixture. Mix, then sift over the flour and stir everything together well to form a wet batter.

Spoon the mixture out into the prepared cake tin and bake in the oven for 50 minutes. Check if it's cooked with a skewer – if not, give it another 5 minutes but don't overdo it (this is a dense cake). Remove from the oven and leave to cool slightly in the tin, then transfer to a wire rack to cool completely.

For the icing, add all the ingredients to the food processor (you may need to sift the icing sugar in if it's rocky), and give it a generous whizz until it looks smooth, glossy and like you want to dive into it. Spread it all over the top and sides of the cooled cake, at least 2 cm (¾ in) thick. Decorate with a few pecans (I do this as a signal to others that the cake contains nuts) before serving.

TIPS

1. As this is a barbecue showstopper, I sometimes bake this cake then wrap it well in plastic wrap and stick it in the freezer until the night before, defrosting in the fridge overnight and adding the icing on party day.

2. If making and icing this cake in advance, don't wrap it directly in plastic wrap as the icing will stick. Instead, refrigerate it before wrapping it up or stick toothpicks into the icing, then lightly wrap around the toothpicks to keep the wrap from touching the icing.

3. You have a fair bit of room to jig the proportions of the icing here, so if the quantities in your containers of cream cheese and/or ricotta are close to the suggested amount, just chuck the whole lot in. In the cake mix, you can switch out the macadamia oil for olive, sunflower, or peanut oil if you wish.

400 G (14 OZ) CARROTS

180 G (6½ OZ/1¾ CUPS) PECANS, PLUS EXTRA TO DECORATE

180 G (6½ OZ) SOFT BROWN SUGAR

100 G (3½ OZ) SUGAR

125 ML (4 FL OZ/½ CUP) MACADAMIA OIL OR OTHER NUT OIL

1 TEASPOON BAKING POWDER

1 TEASPOON BICARBONATE OF SODA (BAKING SODA)

1 TABLESPOON GROUND CINNAMON

½ TEASPOON GROUND NUTMEG

¼ TEASPOON SALT

2 EGGS

100 G (3½ OZ) PLAIN YOGHURT

225 G (8 OZ/1½ CUPS) PLAIN (ALL-PURPOSE) FLOUR

3-CHEESE ICING

250 G (9 OZ) CREAM CHEESE

250 G (9 OZ) RICOTTA

300 G (10½ OZ) MASCARPONE

185 G (6½ OZ/1½ CUPS) ICING (CONFECTIONER'S) SUGAR, SIFTED

100 ML (3½ FL OZ) MAPLE SYRUP

STAINED-GLASS CHRISTMAS CAKE

My mother's friend Lynne Dunoon emailed me this recipe a few years ago out of the blue. I think she must have read my mind and sensed I needed a gift for my mum! Lynne got the recipe from a magazine 40 years ago, and I have stuck to the original formula. It is perfect as it is. Every year I make it for my mother, Yoshiko, who in spite of her Japanese background particularly loves all the nuts and fruit in traditional Christmas baking. Sourcing all the different fruit ingredients is a bit of a pain in the arse, but the actual making is dead simple. Makes 2 cakes (1 for me, 1 for posting to Yoshiko)

Cooking time: 2 hours | Prep time: 15 minutes

Preheat the oven to 140°C (275°F). Line two 24 × 14 cm (9½ × 5½ in) loaf (bar) tins with baking paper.

Combine the nuts, dates, mixed peel and candied and dried fruit in a large bowl, reserving a few good-looking bits of fruit for decoration.

Sift the flour into a separate bowl together with the baking powder and salt. Stir in the sugar, then tip the lot into the fruit and nut mixture and stir together thoroughly.

Beat the eggs, vanilla and brandy together in another bowl, then stir into the fruit mixture and mix together well.

Spoon the mixture into the prepared tins. (The mix will be extremely stiff but don't stress – it's meant to be like this! There is just enough moisture to hold the fruit and nuts together for cooking.) Press the mixture down to level off the tops and decorate them with the good-looking fruit you saved, then cover loosely with foil and bake for 2 hours, until solid and golden brown on top.

Leave the cakes to cool completely in the tins before turning out. Wrap in foil and store in the fridge until needed (they will keep for 2–3 months). Slice thinly to serve, and hold a slice up to the window to enjoy the stained-glass effect.

225 G (8 OZ/1½ CUPS) BRAZIL NUTS

225 G (8 OZ/1½ CUPS) BLANCHED ALMONDS

225 G (8 OZ/2¼ CUPS) PECANS OR WALNUTS

120 G (4½ OZ/⅔ CUP) PITTED WHOLE DATES

60 G (2 OZ/⅓ CUP) MIXED PEEL (MIXED CANDIED CITRUS PEEL)

105 G (3½ OZ/½ CUP) RED AND GREEN GLACÉ CHERRIES, HALVED

120 G (4½ OZ) GLACÉ PINEAPPLE, CUT INTO BRAZIL NUT–SIZED PIECES

225 G (8 OZ) GLACÉ APRICOTS, HALVED

40 G (1½ OZ/⅓ CUP) SULTANAS (GOLDEN RAISINS)

60 G (2 OZ/½ CUP) RAISINS

110 G (4 OZ/¾ CUP) PLAIN (ALL-PURPOSE) FLOUR

½ TEASPOON BAKING POWDER

½ TEASPOON SALT

165 G (6 OZ/¾ CUP) CASTER (SUPERFINE) SUGAR

3 LARGE EGGS, BEATEN

1 TEASPOON VANILLA PASTE

60 ML (2 FL OZ/¼ CUP) BRANDY

THANK F*CK FOR...

My mum, Yoshiko Stynes, who continues to give me fresh lessons in how to be a great mum and person.

Martin Bendeler, champion, inspiration and sweetheart.

Anouk Ely, Dee Dee Ely, Mercy Mei and mighty Manbaby, the loves of my life.

Bruce Walters and Janine Moller – two people who gave a fuck very early on and helped locate my mojo, which had prolapsed.

My slice of heaven, Carla Mico.

Anyone who ever ate any of my food.

Alex Halls and all the fucking saints who work in childcare.

Two previously published cookbook writers, Jane Kennedy and Indira Naidoo, who so generously shared their insights.

Gaynor Bishop, who made some terrific humans in her own womb.

The creative team behind the book: Jane Willson, Simon Davis, Vaughan Mossop, Chris Chen, secret weapon Vanessa Austin and Arum Shim.

And finally, the sisters; who exist, who are real, and who look out for each other. You guys are fucking legends and I give all my fucks to you.

Published in 2018 by Hardie Grant Books,
an imprint of Hardie Grant Publishing

Hardie Grant Books (Melbourne)
Building 1, 658 Church Street
Richmond, Victoria 3121

Hardie Grant Books (London)
5th & 6th Floors
52–54 Southwark Street
London SE1 1UN

hardiegrantbooks.com

 A Cataloguing-in-Publication entry is available from the catalogue
of the National Library of Australia at www.nla.gov.au

The Zero F*cks Cookbook
ISBN 978 1 74379 394 7

Publishing Director: Jane Willson
Managing Editor: Marg Bowman
Design Manager: Jessica Lowe
Editor: Simon Davis
Designer: Vaughan Mossop, Neighbourhood Creative
Photographer: Chris Chen
Food Stylist: Vanessa Austin
Production Manager: Todd Rechner
Production Coordinator: Tessa Spring

Colour reproduction by Splitting Image Colour Studio
Printed in China by 1010 Printing International Limited